Mopeds

by Paul DuPre

Greatlakes Living Press, Publishers, Matteson, Illinois

Mopeds
© **Greatlakes Living Press** 1977
All rights reserved
Printed in U.S.A.
ISBN: 0-915498-46-4
Library of Congress Catalog Card Number: 77-71568

Cover design by Paul J. Henderson/St. Louis
Other design by Chris Avers

Greatlakes Living Press
21750 Main Street
Matteson, Illinois 60443

Contents

Foreword

The motorized bicycle, or "moped," is a relatively new vehicle in the U.S.A., and it is of the utmost importance that state laws be enacted throughout the country to:

1. define the vehicle separately;
2. remove it from the inappropriate definitions of motor vehicle, motorcycle, motor driven cycle and/or motor scooter found in most state laws;
3. establish operating regulations consistent with the low acceleration, power and speed of the vehicle and the simplicity of its operation (less complicated than the average 10-speed bicycle).

The Motorized Bicycle Association considers it important that the definition of the vehicle include: (a) requirement for fully operative pedals; (b) requirement for an automatic transmission; (c) a maximum design speed of 25 to 30 miles per hour from a maximum engine size of 50 cc, and a maximum brake horsepower.

In terms of operating regulations, the Motorized Bicycle Association recommends that:

1. operation be prohibited on interstate highways, tollroads, limited access highways and sidewalks;
2. minimum age for the operator be established at 14 or 15 years;
3. the motorized bicycle be registered as a bicycle;
4. the operator be subject to all state and local traffic regulations and rules of the road;
5. accident reporting be required in order for accurate records to be maintained.

Restriction of maximum power and speed by definition and the operating regulations suggested above will result in safe operation of motorized bicycles. It also is very important, in the opinion of the Motorized Bicycle Association, that all mopeds be manufactured or modified for sale in the U.S.A. in strict conformity with the Federal Department of Transportation (National Highway Traffic Safety Administration) to equipment standards covering lights, tires, brakes and controls and displays (Federal Motor Vehicle Safety Standards Nos. 108, 119, 122 and 123).

Paul Zimmerman, Executive Director
Motorized Bicycle Association
Washington, D.C.

Introduction

Around 20,000,000 motorized bicycles, usually called "mopeds," are now in use worldwide. For more than 30 years these convenient, inexpensive, easy-to-ride units have furnished cheap, effective transportation throughout Europe, Asia and other parts of the world. They have been a long time crossing the ocean in significant numbers to be sold to automobile-oriented Americans.

Today, however, with the ever-increasing fuel costs, growing concern for the environment and determined efforts to reduce air pollution, vehicles that will get you where you want to go at 25 mph, delivering up to 200 miles on a gallon of gasoline mixed with oil, are beginning to make a lot of sense to a lot of Americans. Naturally, mopeds are not suitable for high-speed highways or toll roads.

As commuting vehicles in fair weather, or even not-so-fair weather with suitable protective clothing, the cost is under two cents per mile for fuel as opposed to about 15 cents and more for most cars. Maintenance costs are extremely low—occasionally a spark plug needs changing, but otherwise these perky little units seem to just keep running with little or no attention. Storage is about the same as for an ordinary bicycle, and they are easily transported.

Mopeds are not motorcycles. They are not as big, powerful, fast, noisy, expensive, heavy or bulky, and accident rates across the world are considerably lower for mopeds than for either cars or motorcycles. Mopeds are not motor scooters. Mopeds are pedal bicycles with additional motor assistance that range in weight from about 60 lbs. to around 100 lbs.

A moped rider needs no special skills or ability—if you can ride a bicycle, a moped presents no problems. There are no gears, clutch, foot-brakes, kick starters or heavy electrical equipment. They are easier to operate than a 10-speed bicycle.

America has been missing out on a long tried-and-tested personal transportation method—one spectacularly low in initial cost and in operating expenses. They are fun, quiet, healthy, and fuel and pollution saving. And they are safe. They relieve traffic congestion and parking problems.

As this book went to press, some 95,000 mopeds have been sold in the U.S.A. during the preceding 12-month period. The industry was anticipating tripling that figure in the following 12 months. Worldwide, in 1976, sales exceeded 4 million units, manufactured by close to 100 companies.

Countries where people depend heavily upon mopeds for short-haul transportation include France, Italy, West Germany, Austria, Spain, Switzerland, Britain, Denmark, Morocco, Algeria, Nigeria, Iran, Japan, Taiwan and Canada (chiefly Ontario and Quebec). Close to 8 million are estimated to be in use in France alone. French authorities consider motorized bicycles so essential to the transportation of workers to and from their jobs that special commuter trains bring commuters *and their mopeds* in and out of

Paris.

Throughout Western Europe and in Canada, mopeds use the same traffic lanes as cars and are subject to the same basic traffic laws. In some countries, mopeds are permitted to use special lanes designed exclusively for bicycle use.

Rapidly rising traffic density is outgrowing street capacity in several European cities (including the important French city of Lyons) and has resulted in proposed legislation to ban private, nonessential cars and motorcycles from streets in the cities' cores. Alternatives that are being officially encouraged are use of public transportation systems, mopeds and bicycles.

Moped enthusiasts in the U.S.A. see the possibility of similar situations developing in some cities in the near future. Of all the alternative methods of commuting from the outskirts of a city to its business district or industrial areas, the moped has more to offer in practicality, economy, convenience and helping solve downtown traffic problems.

Acknowledgments

Because motorized bicycles are still very new in America, this book may not contain full descriptions of all moped models distributed in America. However, the information given will be of value to those interested in this new, economical, enjoyable method of personal transportation.

The book could not have been completed without the valuable assistance given by the Motorized Bicycle Association, Washington, D.C., which furnished statistics, legislation information, projections, names of manufacturers and importers, photographs and other vital assistance.

Our thanks also extend to the Motorcycle Industry Council, Inc., Washington, D.C. for additional statistics and information and to a number of manufacturers' U.S. subsidiaries for their assistance in supplying information about their products and photographs.

The author and publishers owe special gratitude to Steyr Dailmer Puch of Puch America Corporation for special help with and interest in this publication.

1

The
Many Modes
of the Moped

COMMERCIAL APPLICATIONS

It may surprise many of those giving serious consideration to the moped as a convenient, inexpensive means of shorthaul commuting to and from work, to learn that these versatile units have a number of commercial uses. No doubt some of these applications will be discovered by Americans as moped use increases here; some, however, are essentially peculiar to one country or another.

In French cities it is not uncommon to see the traditional onion seller with his body and machine festooned in garlands of his wares, chugging along residential streets ringing a bell or sounding his horn and selling his wares directly from his moped.

In many communities in Holland and in other European countries, police officers and patrolmen find mopeds easier on the legs than walking or bicycling. Police machines are modified to deliver higher speeds and, while they cannot always catch speeding cars, they can overhaul lawbreaking mopeders! They also can work their way easily through traffic jams to determine the problem, scoot down alleys where a car often cannot go and ride easier on rural dirt roads.

In many European country towns and villages, you may see business-suited gentlemen with traditional doctor's black bags strapped to the luggage carriers of their mopeds, buzzing along on their house-call rounds. Doctors, visiting nurses and midwives often rely on mopeds to visit their patients.

Mail is delivered by moped in a great many rural areas. In the U.S.A., some commercial uses for mopeds immediately come to mind as future possibilities. Newsboys, complying with age requirements in various states, could hasten and simplify their tasks on mopeds. Many large cities use messengers on bicycles to make deliveries of special letters, artwork, type proofs, news copy, legal documents, films, small packages, etc. Moped use would enable messenger services to make more deliveries faster and more profitably. Security patrols in large industrial complexes would find mopeds easy on the feet and economical, yet not so fast that the guard would suffer impaired efficiency.

Towing a small trailer or freight box, possible moped applications include drug deliveries; selling ice cream; use by household appliance servicemen, telephone installers and repairmen; use by social workers; use by building inspectors and workmen speeding to remote parts of huge construction sites; for inspecting electric cables for storm damage; for delivering hot pizzas, flowers, etc.

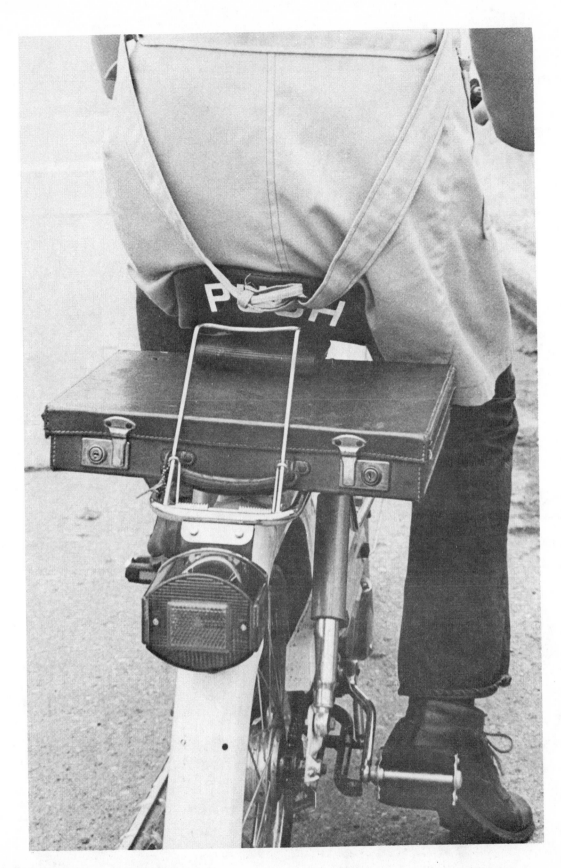

The commuting vehicle of the future.

Paul DuPre

For such tasks, mopeds make a lot of sense. They do not get held up in traffic jams—they may be pushed along the sidewalk, usually with motor assistance to bypass street problems. Even in one of Detroit's gas-gobbling, high-powered monstrosities, you usually cannot achieve more than about 25 mph in city streets because of heavy traffic, pedestrian crossings, traffic signals and laws.

PERSONAL USE

In a great many countries where mopeds have been in use for many years, young people use them extensively to get to and from schools and colleges. They are popular for shopping trips and for calling on friends.

The new fun, easy way to go on quick neighborhood errands is the motorized bicycle. A quick trip to the supermarket is really quick. No more pulling out the four-wheeled gas guzzler to ride a mile to a shopping center and then driving up and down looking for a parking space—all for a couple of bags of groceries. (Photo courtesy of Motobecane.)

Three executives of the Batavus U.S. affiliate company on mopeds.

On a visit to Hong Kong I saw modified mopeds being used in traditional rickshaw fashion, carrying Oriental women on their endless visits to shops, dressmakers, friends or just wishing to be seen abroad.

In Holland, where mopeds are an essential part of the personal transportation scene in all weathers, owners bind nylon cord around the wheels between the spokes at intervals for improved traction on mud, snow, sand and ice.

In Austria, France, Italy, Holland and other countries where mopeds are manufactured and where automobiles and even motorcycles are far out of

Many state parks permit the use of motorized bicycles because of their low noise, low speed and low pollution factors. (Photo courtesy of Steyr-Daimler-Puch.)

the financial reach of the average family, mopeds are the only way for hundreds of thousands of people to get around safely and quickly. Public transportation often is infrequent and poorly scheduled and routed, as in most U.S. towns that have relied too heavily on automobiles.

With gasoline prices in the U.S. rapidly rising to astronomical heights, the Motorized Bicycle Association believes mopeds have a great future for commuting alone, and authorities feel that this use represents by far the biggest share of the moped market.

Their 25-30 mph speed limitations preclude them as highway commuting vehicles for most suburbanites, but for those living on the outer limits of the city, mopeds represent economy, convenience, pleasure and time-saving advantages over public transportation.

Increased use of motorized bicycles by commuters and others will considerably cut our cities' air pollution problems, reduce traffic noise, decrease traffic congestion, reduce the number of cars parked in city streets, relieve overcrowding in parking lots and eliminate many "Sorry—Full" signs at parking garages.

Based on experiences with mopeds in European and Asian countries, where they have been commonplace for many years (and more recently in Canada), moped use in the U.S.A. will cut traffic injuries and fatalities. This in turn will lighten the heavy and ever-increasing burden that traffic accidents place upon emergency rooms of hospitals. Insurance companies will

Boating enthusiasts are discovering that shipping a couple of mopeds aboard gives them cheap transportation at their next port of call. The boaters can use the mopeds to explore or shop. (Photo courtesy of Motobecane.)

save vast sums of their investors' money and will be able to stimulate the economy by investing on a larger scale.

Many of our senior citizens living in retirement communities have already discovered mopeds which, in some cases, are replacing bicycles as a means of visiting friends in other parts of the larger communities; for riding to the golf course, tennis courts, clubhouse, swimming pool, shops, churches, meetings, etc. Or just as a means of "taking the air."

Some retirement communities, especially in the warmer states, are located within easy moped riding distance of shopping centers, social services offices, libraries, beaches and other points that today's active, alert senior citizens must, or like to, visit. Mopeds will see increasing use in such communities, offering a choice of physical exercise by pedaling or motorized riding to one's destinations without physical exertion and without spending money for the high price of gasoline to run the car.

For college and university students in any country motorized bicycles offer a convenient, easy and quick means of commuting between various buildings that are often so far apart that many students actually have to run from one class to another. In France, one college student in four rides a motorized bicycle. Mopeds provide inexpensive transportation from living quarters to the campus and fit the student's budget much more readily than does operating an automobile. Fuel and upkeep costs are extremely low; the units reduce traffic problems and overuse of local city streets that usually occurs near all our ever-expanding colleges.

Campus utilization of motorized bicycles, like commuting to and from work, has long been popular in European countries—not only by students but also by faculty members.

Depending on age restrictions in various states, it seems to be a fair assumption that we will see heavy future use of mopeds by high school students—particularly in states where the legal driving age is 18, whereas mopeds may be ridden at age 16 and even 15 in some states.

Again, the results will be economically beneficial, not only to students and their parents but also to the entire community, since extensive moped use will cut traffic accident injuries and fatalities, reduce traffic congestion and the burden on police departments and hospital emergency rooms, decrease parking problems, save fuel, lower air pollution, reduce traffic noise and provide many other benefits.

The use of mopeds by people who suffer certain physical handicaps must not be overlooked. Those with respiratory, heart and other health problems that might restrict the use of a regular bicycle can often get around comfortably on motorized bicycles—pedaling as much or as little as they desire and are capable of doing.

RECREATIONAL USE

As a new type of recreational vehicle, the moped offers great promise. It is anticipated that many federal and state parks, forests and wildlife preserves will permit use of low-noise, low-speed mopeds on bicycle paths and hiking trails as the leisure riding demand increases with the popularity of the units.

Outdoors enthusiasts can transport their mopeds to remote areas via station wagon, automobile, camping vehicle, trailer, truck, etc. and then can moped/backpack much farther into the wilderness than would be possible on foot. This will relieve the overcrowding in some parks caused by large

Moped use is catching on with the campus crowd. The unit offers an economical way to commute to college and for getting around campus.

numbers of weekend backpackers, the garbage backpackers leave behind or try to bury and other problems caused by large numbers of people using the same few miles of trails.

Using a rear wheel luggage rack, side panniers and one's own back, it is a simple matter on a moped to carry a tent, sleeping bags, camp stove, cooking pots, utensils, food, water, a garbage bag and other camping necessities.

In many European countries it is common to see moped owners enjoying a ride along the beach—sometimes as many as a hundred riders in one group conducting a club activity—that usually includes swimming, picnicking, beach games, sand races and just good old lounging in the sun.

Moped clubs are already forming in California, Florida and other states, and events are being staged, including long and short distance racing, enduro rides, rallies, obstacle courses, hill climbing and mud-and-sand races and other activities. The Dutch, who are credited with inventing skating, have lake and river races on the ice, including moped ice hockey. They

The moped is an enjoyable and economical way to reach the tennis courts. You can pedal or let the motor work while you relax and enjoy the scenery.

use mopeds with wheels wrapped with nylon cord for increased traction. In Europe you can also buy special spiked tires for ice riding (they are illegal on the roads and streets).

In Britain moped polo is becoming popular as a participant and spectator sport. Manipulating a moped while playing polo calls for extreme skill—as much as is required to manipulate and control a polo pony.

Essentially an American sport, snowmobile use is not very popular in Europe. But many European motorized bicycle owners like to ride the snow-clad trails in woods, forests, and on open fields, as well as country roads, wearing ski suits. This recreational use of mopeds is their equivalent to our ever-growing sport of snowmobiling.

In many parts of the U.S.A., water-sports enthusiasts will soon be taking their mopeds aboard for use on sightseeing trips and shopping expeditions at their ports of call or on the other side of a lake.

It is safe to assume that as more foreign-built mopeds are sold in this country and more companies realize the profit potential of these economical and practical units, Americans will adopt many European uses for the moped besides basic commuting.

The Motorized Bicycle Association and the Motorcycle Industry Council do not anticipate that use of mopeds will cause reduced sales in motorcycles—the two vehicles are too dissimilar and are designed and built for different purposes. Similarly, bicycle manufacturers do not regard the growing interest in mopeds as a threat to their business since the moped serves different needs and desires. Although a moped may be pedaled, you would not want to pedal one for any great length of time, uphill, or to attain speed. Using a 10-speed bicycle, any reasonably good bicyclist can achieve greater speed than with a moped. There seems little possibility that federal regulations will ever permit construction or sale of mopeds with higher-powered motors that could bring them more in line with light motorcycles.

Thus, the moped has finally reached the U.S.A. and is rapidly gaining acceptance and popularity for many uses, just as it entered the European scene soon after World War II. At that time the U.S. economy was considerably healthier than today. Today, new cars—even compacts—are priced beyond the means of a great many families who could have afforded them a few years ago. Gasoline is rapidly becoming an expensive luxury that will gradually reduce automobile use. People will have to think carefully before burning expensive fuel in a 4,000-pound automobile to get a newspaper, loaf of bread, package of cigarettes, etc., from a store two blocks away.

The moped with the "big wheel."

2

Moped Models

Although there are close to 100 manufacturers of mopeds throughout the world, mostly in European countries, relatively few are exporting motorized bicycles to the U.S.A. in any quantity at the time of this book's publication.

For the most part, these manufacturers have American affiliates that import and distribute their products. The majority of these affiliate companies are members of the Motorized Bicycle Association, headquartered at 1001 Connecticut Avenue, N.W., Washington, D.C.

The following is a list of the principal companies currently distributing mopeds on behalf of their overseas manufacturers. Following the address is the brand name of each distributor's unit.

American Jawa, Ltd., East, 185 Express Street, Plainview, L.I., New York 11803—BABETTA

American Jawa, Ltd., West, 18408 Laurel Park Road, Compton, California 90224—BABETTA

Canadian affiliates: C-Z & Jawa Motors Canada Ltd., 268 Royal York Road, Toronto, and C-Z & Jawa Motors Canada Ltd., 7600 Trans-Canada Highway, Montreal, Quebec—BABETTA

Batavus USA, 2546 Northeast Expressway, Atlanta, Georgia 30345—BATAVUS

Bermuda Bikes, Inc., 606 Ocean Avenue, Point Pleasant, New Jersey 08742—BERMUDA BIKES

Cimatti, Ltd., International Sales Division, 68 Sugar Hollow Road, Danbury, Connecticut 06810—CITY BIKE

Columbia Manufacturing Co., 1 Cycle Street, Westfield, Massachusetts 01085—COLUMBIA

Cycles Peugot [USA], Inc., 540 East Alondra, Gardena, California 90247—PEUGOT

F.G.S. Enterprises, Inc., Atlas Terminal Building, 8000 Cooper Avenue, Glendale, New York—INTRAMOTOR

Grycner Motors Corporation, Moped Division, 301 Tamarisk Road, Palm Springs, California—SMILY

Malaguti of America, Inc., 1851 Post Road, Warwick, Rhode Island 02886—MALAGUTI

Motobecane America Ltd., 86 Orchard Street, Hackensack, New Jersey 07601—MOTOBECANE

Motor Bikes Import, 6007 S. Rte. 30, Pennsauken, New Jersey 08105—SAFARI

Motorized Bicycles Imports, Inc., Sgt. Jasper Building, Charleston, South Carolina 29401—CITY BIKE

North America Tradimpex Corp., 1938 New Highway, Farmingdale, New York 11735—PALOMA

Portofino International, Inc., 1107 Broadway, New York, New York 10010—PACER

Steyr Daimler Puch of America Corporation, Box 7777, Greenwich, Connecticut—PUCH MAXI

Tomos America, Inc., 553 North Irby Street, Florence, South Carolina 29503—TOMOS

Velosolex America, Ltd. [a subsidiary of Motobecane], 86 Orchard Street, Hackensack, New Jersey 07601—VELOSOLEX

Vespa of America Corporation, 322 E. Grand Avenue, South San Francisco, California 94080—CIAO, BRAVO

Lightweight and compact, the moped is easily loaded onto a boat for later use at lakeside stops.

Mechanical specifications on all units to be sold in the U.S.A. were not available at the time of publication, nor were photographs of all U.S. units.

The following presents details of some motorized bicycles that are presently being sold in America or will be sold here soon.

ANGEL

Specifications for this new moped from Taiwan are the same as those for the Bermuda models (page 18). Differences are:

Engine— 48cc 2-stroke, reed valve with 7:1 compression ratio. Transmission is the same automatic two-stage type; wheels have 2:00-17" tires and hub brakes front and rear. Swing arm and shock absorbers comprise the suspension system on both wheels; electric power is supplied by a 6-volt battery and a Bosch magneto. Standard equipment on the Angel moped includes front fork lock, speedometer, turn signals, electric horn, sealed beam headlight, tail/stop light, tool kit, reserve fuel supply, front and rear luggage carriers, rear view mirror and deluxe sprung saddle. Options include speed and horsepower limitations to meet state requirements. The engine delivers up to 150 miles per gallon.

BABETTA

Built in Czechoslovakia, the sturdy Babetta is imported by American Jawa Ltd., with two main U.S. offices and two locations in Canada. American Jawa Ltd., East, is at 185 Express Street, Plainview, Long Island, New York 11803; American Jawa Ltd., West, is at 18408 Laurel Park Road, Drawer 15, Compton, California 90224. The Canadian affiliates are: C-Z & Jawa Motors Canada Ltd., 268 Royal York Road, Toronto, and C-Z & Jawa Motors Canada Ltd., 7600 Trans-Canada Highway, Montreal, Quebec.

The Babetta features an air-cooled, two-stroke, 50 cc engine, with connecting rod mounted in a needle bearing. Transmission is via an automatic centrifugal clutch and single speed gears with shafts in ball bearings. The carburetor is a Jikov 2909 model with starting device, and the ignition is fully transistorized.

The frame is fully welded tubular steel, and the unit has solid hub brakes, front and rear, telescopic front fork, rear swinging arm and shock absorbers. The fuel tank is integral with the frame, and the unit is designed to deliver a minimum of 130 mpg. The total weight is 97 pounds.

BATAVUS

Founded in 1904, the Dutch Firm Batavus is the largest manufacturer of two-wheeled vehicles in Holland, where millions rely on this type of transportation rather than on cars. The company produces over 3,000,000 bicycles and motorized bicycles a year, exporting large numbers to many other countries.

The American subsidiary, responsible for importing Batavus mopeds into the United States of America, is Batavus USA, Inc., 2546 Northeast Expressway, Atlanta, Georgia 30345.

Three models of the Batavus moped are currently being marketed throughout the U.S.A.: the **VA-Standard,** the **VA-Deluxe** and the **HS-50 De-luxe**. Only the "top-of-the-line" HS-50 Deluxe model has much in the way of visual or mechanical difference.

The basic Batavus moped has a single-tube frame with a detachable fuel tank capable of holding .95 gallons (1.3 gallons for the HS-50). Engine lubrication, as in most two-stroke engines, is accomplished by the small amount of oil mixed with gasoline that forms the fuel (40 parts gasoline to 1 part oil for the first 500 miles; 50:1 after 500 miles).

A 48 cc engine provides motorized power assistance, utilizing an Encarwi carburetor. Transmission is one speed with automatic centrifugal clutch; rear drive is by means of a 1/2-inch x 3/16-inch chain. The unit has front and rear fully internal hub drumbrakes; the front wheel has telescopic fork suspension, and the rear suspension is sustained by swing arm and shock absorbers.

Additional features include illuminated speedometer/odometer, rear luggage carrier with spring clip, electric horn, front and rear indicators (standard on the Deluxe and HS-50 models only), tough Durolon epoxy resin paint finish, Niros chrome plating, motor kill switch, tool kit and box and others. The firm offers a wide range of accessories similar to those offered by other makes.

The Batavus model VA.

The Batavus model HS-50.

BERMUDA

About 150 years ago a Flemish blacksmith named Alexander Claeys, in Zedelgem, Belgium, was busy doing his thing when suddenly he became quite ambitious and founded a company known then as A. Claeys Flandria. The family firm repaired, renovated and built a wide range of metal products. In 1896 the company went into the bicycle manufacturing business and after World War II added motorized bicycles to its line. The company produced 25,000 mopeds in 1950—its first year of moped production. The plant's assembly line now has a capacity of 300 motorized bicycles a day. The firm has stayed a family concern—the president is now Mr. Paul Claeys.

In addition to their popularity in Europe, Bermuda mopeds are familiar to tourists to that island paradise and for many years these handsome and economical vehicles have been praised as the best, most leisurely, least exhausting way to see and feel the charm of Bermuda. The moped makes Bermuda's many scenic hills and dales child's play to people who couldn't tackle them on an ordinary pedal bicycle. The cost of renting a moped and buying fuel for it in Bermuda makes this by far the most economical way of seeing the island, as well as the most pleasurable.

The Bermuda moped.

The Robert Bosch people have provided a magneto with sufficient generating capacity to meet the needs of the NHTSA-required sealed beam headlight, the stop light, tail light, electric horn and ignition system on units imported into the U.S.A.

The 49 cc engine, made by the Belgian company, Flandria, is a single-cylinder, two-stroke motor with a cast iron cyclinder, chrome alloy piston and carefully balanced, roller bearing crank shaft. The engine is mounted ahead of the pedal crank and provides a very low center of gravity. As with most mopeds, you use the pedals to get the engine started and to give it a little extra help on the hills. The engine drives the unit through a dual centrifugal clutch—the inner clutch is connected to the rear wheel and is thus activated by forward motion, while the outer clutch is connected to the engine and is brought into action by engine rpm's. As you pedal to get started (either moving along or while the vehicle is still on the stand), the inner clutch pads expand and transfer rotary motion to the outer clutch attached to the engine. With the decompressor open, there is sufficient drag to turn over the engine. Closing the decompressor permits the engine to fire on compression and start up. When the engine is idling, there is not enough centrifugal force being generated to activate the outer clutch and, since the bike is at rest, the inner clutch is not being activated and so there is no forward movement.

To start off on your Bermuda (as with most other mopeds) after pedaling a short distance, you open the handlebar throttle and the increased rpm causes the outer clutch to become engaged. As sufficient speed is attained the wheel revolutions, in turn, bring the inner clutch to bear and then both clutches are in full operation. As you slow down to stop, the outer clutch automatically disengages as wheel revolutions slow down and the engine is then back to the idling mode. This two-stage type of automatic clutching system, designed for safety, is incorporated in some other makes of motorized bicycle and there are indications that before long this will be a standard moped feature. The safety factor is that through this double clutch system, you cannot make a sudden jack-rabbit start that could throw you off balance and put your moped temporarily out of control.

The U.S. firm importing and marketing Bermuda mopeds is Bermuda Bikes, Inc., 606 Ocean Avenue, Point Pleasant, New Jersey 08742. In spring of 1977, three models of the Bermuda moped were being sold in those U.S. states that had approved and devised laws affecting the sale and operation of mopeds. Descriptions of the units are given below.

The Hamilton

Engine: 2-cycle, 49.7 cc, with a 7.5:1 compression ratio. Maximum speed: 25 mph and the machine is designed to climb an 11.7 percent grade without pedaling. The engine delivers approximately 133 miles per gallon and produces 1.4 maximum horsepower at 5,500 rpm. The tank holds one U.S. gallon. Fuel is regular gasoline and oil mixture (4 percent oil). Frame is pressed steel and the unit has telescopic front forks and rigid rear forks. The wheels have drum brakes front and rear. Net weight of the Hamilton is 92 lbs. Equipment includes sealed beam adjustable headlight, 18-watt SAE Standard stoplight with a 5-watt tail light, electric horn, Bosch W145T1 spark plug, tool kit, safety flag. This model comes in blue and white.

The Hampton

All specifications and equipment for the Hampton model are the same as for the Hamilton with the exception of an added speedometer/odometer, a swinging-arm-type rear suspension with shock absorbers, steering column lock, a 7/10th inch longer wheelbase, a 97-lb. net weight, and a slight difference in tire size. Both the Hamilton and the Hampton are available in lower power and lower speed versions where required by state laws.

CIMATTI

The Cimatti Company has long been an important factor in the industrial economy of Italy. They are world-renowned manufacturers of all types of motorcycles—their units have won races, endurance events, obstacle competitions and other competitive events in various countries for many years. Recently the company added mopeds to its line of motorized two-wheeled vehicles. Cimatti mopeds are sold all over Europe and Asia and now are being distributed throughout North America by Cimatti Ltd., 68 Sugar Hollow Road, Danbury, Connecticut 06810. The American firm has a nationwide distribution system that incorporates some 750 dealerships. In addition, the company intends to establish dealerships with full servicing facilities and trained mechanics in other states that are expected during 1977 to pass legislation permitting the use of motorized bicycles on their streets.

City Bike

The City Bike uses the popular and reliable Minarelli engine. This engine is used by most Italian and many non-Italian moped and motorcycle manufacturers and is considered about the best engine available today for this type of application. It is a single-cylinder, two-stroke, 49.6 cc, piston-port type, which is probably the simplest and least trouble-free of all engines of its kind. It has only three moving parts and has ports instead of valves to admit fresh fuel, regulate the mixture and vent out the burned gases.

As with all two-stroke engines, firing occurs every 360 degrees as the piston reaches the top (second-stroke) position. This is why these engines are called two-stroke or two-cycle—one stroke downward after firing and a return to the top position for refiring. The engine uses an NGK-B6HS spark plug, a Bosch U145T1, or an equivalent Champion. The gap must be exactly .024".

The fuel tank is mounted behind the seat and holds 2-1/4 quarts, but the company supplies an optional auxiliary tank that mounts on the front frame member and holds 1-1/2 gallons. This total (with the optional tank) gives the Cimatti City Bike the longest range on one fill-up of fuel and makes the City Bike particularly popular as a rental unit, especially in Hawaii where the units are frequently out for a full day or longer at one time. Fuel used is Minarelli synthetic oil that is supplied already mixed in 4-oz. bottles, at a ratio of 64 parts gasoline to one part oil.

The transmission is a single-speed, automatic oil-bath clutch type with handlebar-mounted engagement lever and chain drive to the rear sprocket. The chain should neither be too tight or too loose. It should have about 1/2" of play, tested at the lower center portion of the chain.

The suspension system incorporates telescopic front forks with drop-out lugs and swinging arm with heavy-duty shock absorbers on the rear forks, providing a very comfortable ride.

The City Bike frame is made of heavy-gauge tubular steel. The fuel tank is mounted beneath the rear luggage carrier, giving the frame a clean, bicycle-type appearance (without the optional frame-mounted fuel tank). The wheels have heavy-duty chrome rims and use 2-1/4 x 16-inch tires on both wheels. The City Bike has hub brakes, front and rear.

Additional equipment includes a sealed-beam, adjustable headlamp, with a built-in illuminated speedometer and side reflectors, rearview mirror and additional footrests for use when the moped is in the motor-assisted mode. Various options are available from City Bike dealerships.

COLUMBIA

Columbia Manufacturing Company is the first U.S. company to manufacture mopeds. This 100-year-old American firm, headquartered in Westfield, Massachusetts, is now a division of MTD Products, Inc., of Cleveland, Ohio. The founder of Columbia, Albert Augustus Pope, was an outstanding business genius and was one of the first Americans to see the potential of manufacturing and mass-marketing bicycles. By 1900, based on a number of innovations, he had established a wide-spread industrial empire. His company was the first in the world to develop a system of uniform interchangeable parts for bicycles and to perfect and use adjustable ball bearings. It was then the largest bicycle manufacturing company in the world, employing the phenomenal number of 10,000 workers. Columbia was the first to make the change from solid to pneumatic tires. Pope pioneered vast improvements in drop forging, metal turning, steel hardening, steel tubing manufacturing and metal plating.

Through adult tricycle production, Columbia pioneered and perfected the rear end differential, front wheel differential steering and rolled and curved steel wheel rims. In 1877, then a manufacturer of various metal items, Pope saw English high-wheel bicycles at the Philadelphia Centennial Exposition and immediately decided that this product would bring him fame and fortune. Soon, Columbia bicycles were being sold throughout the world as quickly as the manufacturing facility could build them. The company now builds and sells bicycles under two brand names—Columbia and Gold Crest—heading a long list of products, with the new addition of motorized bicycles rounding off the list under the brand name *Commuter*.

Commuter

The Commuter has a reinforced unitized frame with integral tank and chrome filler cap; a Sachs 505/1, two-cycle, horizontal cylinder, chrome-faced engine of 48 cc displacement; and a Bosch 6-V, 20-W/5-W/10-W magneto. The engine uses a fuel mixture of 50 parts regular gasoline to one part oil; the tank holds 3.5 quarts with reserve and delivers up to 150 miles per gallon.

The Commuter was the first moped built by an American company for sale in the United States. The Commuter's maker, the Columbia Manufacturing Company, has long been one of the leaders in bicycle production.

The transmission is secondary drive with #420 heavy-duty chain, single-speed gear and automatic centrifugal clutch. The front fork is cross-braced with chrome telescopic shock absorber and security lock, and the rear suspension is swing arm with chrome telescopic shock absorber. Other features include front and rear drum brakes, large, black enamel 18-W sealed beam headlight, rectangular black enamel 5-W tail light, 10-W stop light, luggage carrier, double-leg kick stand, speedometer-odometer, electric horn and rear-view mirror with adjustable arm.

The Commuter's overall length is 70 inches, 38 inches high and the dry weight is 100 pounds.

GARELLI

Around the turn of the century, the Agrati and Garelli families in Monticello, Italy, formed a production company that soon split into two separate firms. The Agrati brothers began producing parts and accessories for bicycle manufacturers, and the Garelli group concentrated on building motorcycles.

The Agrati firm became one of the world's leading suppliers to the bicycle manufacturing industry, and the excellent 350 cc motorcycle made by the Garelli group set world records that remained unbroken for many years.

The two companies again merged after World War II and began to specialize in motorcycles of the 50 cc class and in mopeds. Dealers for Agrati-Garelli products have been established in Boston, New York, Newton, Salt Lake City, San Francisco and Los Angeles, as well as other American cities. Dealers are also found in Europe, Asia, Africa and Oceania.

Only four of the many motorcycles that the firm terms "motorized cycles" can be defined as mopeds, or motorized bicycles, under the National Highway Traffic Safety Administration classification.

The Sport

New for 1977, the Sport uses the famed Garelli engine, used by many manufacturers of equipment of various kinds across the world that need this type of engine. Garelli's two-stroke, 49 cc alloy head engine has been used successfully to power much heavier, two-wheeled bicycles in the motorcycle category and a variety of other equipment. The carburetor is a Dell'Orto Type SHA 14/12.

The single-speed transmission incorporates a centrifugal clutch system and reduction gears in oil bath—the rear wheels are chain driven. Like most mopeds, this unit is started by pedaling.

The tubular steel frame incorporates the step-through feature popular with most moped makes. The fenders are stainless steel and the chain cover is pressed steel. The rear carrier includes an integral toolbox, with necessary tools, plus brackets for wire side baskets.

Telescopic front forks and swing-arm, helical spring rear forks provide the suspension system.

The electrical system consists of a flywheel magneto, sealed beam headlight, 6-volt tail light (with additional reflector) and an electric horn drawing 24 volts.

The wheels use 3.00 x 10" tires and both wheels have drum brakes. The Garelli 1977 Sport, without additional equipment or fuel, weighs 101 lbs.

American Agrati-Garelli's Sport, one of the five 1977 models, has rubber motor mounts and thicker engine casings for quiet operation. This budget model also comes with larger main bearings, an advanced fluid clutch with brass bushings, a higher voltage electric system with a hotter spark for easier starting and telescopic front suspension.

and is 65 inches in total length.

A standard rear rack, steering column lock, and various options make the Garelli Sport a very pleasant motorized bicycle to own and ride.

The 1977 Grand Sport Deluxe

This model uses a Garelli-built 49 cc two-stroke engine with cast iron horizontal cylinder, radial cooling fins and a die-cast aluminum head. The Dell-'Orto Type SHA 14/12 carburetor with semi-automatic cold start plunger. Compression ratio is 1:7.5.

The tubular steel frame is the same as that used for the Sport; the fuel tank (built integrally with the toolbox under the rear carrier) holds about a gallon of fuel at a mixture ratio of 97:3 and delivers around 150 mpg.

Other differences between this model and the Sport include 2-1/4 x 16" tires, standard speedometer/odometer. A wide range of options make this one of the sportier and most useful mopeds on the market.

INTRAMOTOR GLORIA

Intramotor Gloria, headquartered in Verona, Italy, is currently importing two motorized bicycles into the U.S.A. through F.G.S. Enterprises, Inc., 8000 Cooper Avenue, Glendale, New York. The manufacturing company lists its capital at $2.5 million. Both units being imported by F.G.S. Enterprises meet all U.S. government standards. Products made by Intramotor Gloria include bicycles, motorized bicycles, motorcross cycles, motorcarts, various accessories and parts, aluminum radiators for home and industry and other items.

With its present manufacturing facilities, the company can produce some 100,000 motorized bicycles per year.

Specifications of the company's two models of mopeds—The Blanco and the Scout are as follows.

The Blanco

The Blanco has a frame of heavy-gauge stamped steel with integral fuel tank, stamped front wheel fork with spring suspension or floating drag links, floating fork with shock absorbers on rear wheel, 16-inch diameter wheels, front and rear hub brakes, cylinder cubic centimeter displacement

The Intramotor-Gloria Blanco.

is 49.6—engine is cooled by a combination of air flow and forced air. The carburetor is a Dell'Orto SHW 14-12; the flywheel magnetor alternator is 23-W, 6-V; spark plugs are thermal-rated at 225. Basic equipment includes sealed beam headlight, stop-tail light, electric horn, gas tank cap and tap, choke lever, automatic clutch in oil bath with handlebar control, chain drive automatic single-gear transmission, hand accelerator and brakes, three-quart fuel capacity using a 20 to one gasoline-oil mixture and delivering up to 180 miles per gallon. The unit weighs 98 pounds and is started by one of two methods—either by pedaling and then engaging the clutch (using choke if engine or air is particularly cold) or with moped on stand, pedaling quickly and engaging the clutch (using the choke if necessary).

The Scout

The Scout has a high-strength steel piping frame, front wheel telescopic fork with shock absorber and floating type forks, 16-inch wheels, front and rear hub brakes, cast-iron cylinder (two-cycle, 49 cc cooled by direct air flow), Dell'Orto SHW 14-12 carburetor, flywheel magneto alternator (23-W, 6-V), spark plugs thermally rated at 225, spirally geared main shaft. Basic equipment includes sealed beam headlight, stop-tail light, electric horn, gas tank cap and tap, choke lever, automatic clutch in oil bath with handlebar control. Starting methods are the same as for the Blanco.

A variety of accessories may be purchased for these two units, including rear luggage rack, baskets, pannier-type saddle bags, rear-view mirror and choice of baked enamel colors. The unit weighs 98 pounds.

The Intramotor-Gloria Scout

The large basket mounted over the rear wheel of mopeds can hold two bags of groceries.

This fisherman found an isolated stream inaccessible to autos.

MALAGUTI

The Malaguti manufacturing concern was established about 40 years ago by Antonio Malaguti—a well known, young sportsman and racing cyclist. The firm enjoys an international reputation for its lightweight bicycles and motorcycles, and in recent years its mopeds have sold well throughout Europe.

The North American affiliate, responsible for distribution of Malaguti motorized bicycles throughout the U.S.A., is Malaguti of America, Inc., 1851 Post Road, Warwick, Rhode Island 02886. An extensive network of dealers has been established along the eastern seaboard and the company is expanding its outlets to cover all states that permit moped use.

The Malaguti moped has an integral fuel tank and a sturdy, stepthrough design frame. The engine is a Morini 2-stroke, 49 cc, 1.3 Bhp with a Dell'-Orto 14/12 carburetor. It uses a 20:1 mixture of gasoline and oil (16:1 during the first 600 miles run-in). The engine utilizes the Bosch WG175T30 spark plug (or equivalent). A 6-volt, 23-watt output magneto-generator supplies the electric power for the sealed-beam adjustable headlight, electric horn, ignition and tail-stop light. Power transmission is by automatic, single-speed clutch and is driven by a single chain. The hub brakes are of the single leading shoe type, front and rear. Both tires are 2.25 x 16", wheelbase is 3' 4-1/2" and overall length of the machine is 5'2".

Malaguti Commuter.

A choke is incorporated into the carburetor with the control lever facing forward on the carburetor on the right side of the engine. The lever is easily reached through an opening in the right footboard. When the throttle is fully opened, the choke is automatically released. The choke is designed only for cold starts—it should not be used when the engine is warm.

The start lever is under the lefthand brake lever on the handlebars and there is an engine stop switch on the right handlebar. The engine is started in the same manner as those of most modern mopeds—move the engine stop switch to the RUN position, turn fuel tap to ON, engage choke and start pedaling. When good momentum has been reached through pedaling, you engage the engine start lever, open the throttle to about halfway (release the engine start lever as soon as the engine starts), and stop pedaling. The unit delivers up to 200 miles per gallon.

The suspension system on the Malaguti consists of heavy-duty telescopic front forks and rear swing arm shock absorbers on the back forks. The seat is very well sprung and heavily padded.

Other features include a steering column lock, high-gloss enamel paint, and a wide range of optional equipment including rearview mirror, windshield, leg shields, saddle bags, directional signals and others. The Malaguti's dry weight is approximately 100 pounds.

MOTOBECANE

Six basic models of Motobecane are produced at the huge five-million-square-foot manufacturing complex of Les Ateliers de la Motobecane in France. In 1923 this company began manufacturing motorcycles. Later, bicycles were added to the product line, and in 1949 the first Motobecane motorized bicycles were produced. Since then, the firm has sold well over 20 million units, becoming the largest manufacturer of motorized bicycles in the world. The company now produces over one million units a year that it sells and services in over 40 countries.

The company's U.S. operations are conducted by Motobecane America Ltd., a subsidiary of the parent company now known as Motobecane S.A. France. The American firm is headquartered in Hackensack, New Jersey and maintains West Coast offices in Los Angeles, California. Warehouse facilities and service training centers are found in both cities, and additional warehouses are located in Cleveland, Ohio; Galveston, Texas; Charleston, South Carolina and Honolulu, Hawaii.

Brief specifications on each of the six principal models of Motobecane mopeds follow (the numbers in parentheses refer to the numbers on the accompanying photographs):

Model 50VL [1]

Motobecane Model 50VL has a variator (variable ratio drive) that helps maintain speed on hills. Telescopic front fork and rear swing-arm suspension and shock absorbers deliver a smooth, sturdy ride. The unit has a stainless steel front fender, heavy chrome-finished rear luggage carrier and side luggage racks, front and rear drum brakes, sealed beam headlight, electric horn, lighted speedometer, steering column lock, engine stop switch, fuel tank tap with reserve capacity, tool kit, tire pump and extra storage compartment.

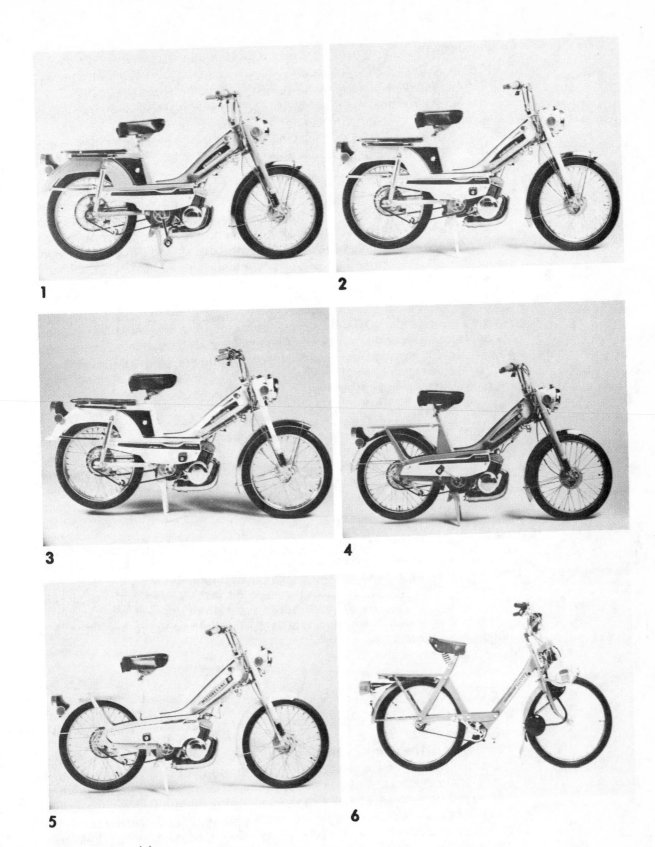

Motobecane models.

Model 50L [2]

Motobecane Model 50L has telescopic front fork and rear swing-arm suspension, shock absorbers, and front and rear drum brakes, stainless steel front fender, chrome luggage carrier and chrome side luggage racks, steering column lock, lighted speedometer, sealed beam headlight, electric horn, engine stop switch, fuel tank tap with reserve capacity, tire pump, tool kit and extra storage compartment.

Model 50S [3]

Motobecane Model 50S has telescopic front fork and rear swing-arm suspension, shock absorbers and front and rear drum brakes, antirust baked enamel fenders, sealed beam headlight, electric horn, engine stop switch, fuel tank tap and reserve capacity, tire pump, tool kit and extra storage compartment. It has provisions for optional steering column lock and speedometer.

Model 40TL [4]

Motobecane Model 40TL has a telescopic front fork and fixed rear suspension, front and rear drum brakes, stainless steel fenders, sealed beam headlight, steering column lock, electric horn, engine stop switch, fuel tank tap with reserve capacity and tool kit. The unit has provisions for optional steering column lock and speedometer.

Model 40TS [5]

Motobecane Model 40TS has telescopic front fork and rear suspension, front and rear drum brakes, high-gloss antirust baked enamel finish, sealed beam headlight, electric horn, tire pump, engine stop switch and fuel tank tap with reserve capacity and tool kit. The unit has provisions for steering column lock and speedometer.

The Horse [6]

The Motobecane Horse was one of the world's first motorized bicycles and remains a big seller. The Horse features an engine mounted above the front wheel driven by a friction roller device. This motor is designed to deliver over 200 miles per gallon. The Horse is 66 inches long and weighs 68 pounds. It has fixed suspension front and rear, front caliper brakes and rear drum brake, sealed beam headlight, stop-tail light, electric horn, tool kit, luggage carrier and tire pump.

PEUGEOT

The French company, Peugeot, has been well known in the U.S.A. for many years because of its well engineered and strongly built automobiles and motorcycles. The Peugeot brand name on bicycles is perhaps not as well known, although they have been sold in this country for a number of years.

The company has been in business for over 100 years—its earlier production was in the areas of tools, household implements and various other metal items. Believing in the future of the bicycle, the company's board of directors started making bicycles in 1885. Four years later, the first Peugeot motorcycles came off the production line. Peugeot motorcycles have achieved great success in competitive events, including a number of world records.

The Peugeot model 103-LVS-U3.

Following World War I, the firm felt the need to form a separate organization, the Cycles Peugeot. Thirty years ago, Cycles Peugeot started producing motorized bicycles and the firm now is the second largest manufacturer of mopeds in the world.

The U.S. subsidiary, Cycles Peugeot (USA), Inc., at 540 East Alondra Boulevard, Gardena, California 90247, is now marketing Peugeot mopeds throughout the U.S.

The Peugeot moped model 103-LVS-U3 conforms to all existing federal, California and Nevada state regulations and models will be modified to meet requirements of other states. The model being marketed on the West Coast has a top speed of 30 mph that is unacceptable in many other states where limits for these units have been set at 20 or 25 mph. It is hoped that all of the states eventually will agree on a standard set of regulations to apply to all motorized bicycles.

A Peugeot 49 cc, two-stroke engine provides the power assistance. The engine is cast-aluminum and the cylinder is chrome-lined; the clutch is the automatic, variable-speed type that requires no gear changing. The telescopic front fork is chromed as are the double suspension rear forks, with shock absorbers. The Peugeot has front and rear drum brakes, Michelin tires mounted on Rigida dimpled rims. The sealed beam headlight, rear-stop light and horn are powered by a Peugeot 6-V, 3-W flywheel magneto.

Other features of this unit include a 1.05-gallon fuel tank, with reserve, giving a range of 135-140 miles; stainless steel front fender, tool kit, luggage carrier, speedometer, front fork security lock, kickstand and five-way reflectors. Peugeot's 103-LVS-U3 comes in fire red and ocean blue. The company is offering two other models that have only slight variations and an impressive list of accessories.

PUCH

At the age of 12, Johann Puch, fascinated by machinery of any kind, ran away from home and led a very colorful life for a few years that included agricultural and mechanical work, some military service and a lengthy mechanics apprenticeship.

In 1885 an extraordinary new invention from England was becoming the rage of the wealthy carriage set of fashionable Europe. It was the so-called "penny-farthing" bicycle, one of the least aesthetic, clumsiest, most difficult to operate, impractical and dangerous wheeled devices ever invented. Puch decided to improve upon the mechanics and engineering of the "penny-farthing."

Investing his savings, he opened a bicycle repair shop, and began build-

The Maxi, Puch's standard moped, has independent suspension, a speedometer and comes in a wide range of colors.

ing his own bicycles—his was the first low-frame unit with same-size wheels, driven by a chain.

Puch bicycles set many world records over the years. He built a few automobiles, and in 1903 his motorcycles came off the production line. These machines, like his bicycles, began collecting trophies all over the world—their design incorporated many unusual features.

Puch's first moped, built in 1904, was more of a pedal-assisted motorcycle than a motorized bicycle. However, since it could be either pedaled or run off the engine, as is the case of a modern motorized bicycle, the "Puch-Motorkerekpar" certainly was one of the first mopeds ever made.

Today the Puch moped is the market leader in England, Denmark, Finland, Holland, Switzerland and Austria. The firm markets well over 200,000 motorized bicycles annually—total sales have exceeded 1,000,000 units.

Under the brand name Puch Maxi, the Steyr Daimler Puch of America Corporation, Box 7777, Greenwich, Connecticut 06830, is marketing seven models of the Austrian company's motorized bicycles.

All have all-welded steel frames of which the fuel tank is an integral part. Maxis have all-chain drive rather than trouble-prone belts found on some European units. A separate chain drive makes pedaling almost effortless. A semi-automatic choke makes for easy starts in cold weather. The speedometer and tail light are rubber-mounted to lessen vibration and impact damage.

Regarded as the elite among mopeds, the Puch Newport model is also economical. The model features hand-painted detailing and reflective tires.

The motor is a 49 cc single-cylinder, two-stroke internal combustion engine that delivers up to 150 miles per gallon of regular gas. The cylinder is chrome-plated, and the engine features a Bosch ignition system and a Bing carburetor. The Maxi has full-width front and rear brakes and telescopic front suspension and rear suspension with twin shock absorbers. Positive-traction Austrian-made Semperit tires are standard on Puch Maxis. The Maxi has automatic transmission in oil bath.

Other features of the Puch Maxi include a built-in tool kit and tire pump; spring-loaded rear carrier; built-in chrome carrying handles for easy carrying and lifting by two persons; low noise level, chrome-plated exhaust; steering lock; sealed beam headlight and others. The company offers a wide range of accessories.

Starting and riding a Puch Maxi is as easy as riding an ordinary bicycle—easier than riding some of the more complicated, multigear bicycles. The first thing to do is to flip the fuel lever, then push in the primer. Now, squeeze the start lever, press on the pedal and release the lever, mounting at the same time. Now you're on your way on one of the better-built mopeds available in the U.S.A. today.

For the hot-rodding moped rider, the Puch Maxi-Sport is equipped with mag wheels, elongated seat and an integrated luggage carrier.

For impromptu picnics or week-long camping trips, mopeds carry everything from a small picnic basket to tents, sleeping bags and other necessary gear.

The moped is an ideal vehicle for an afternoon ride through parks, forest preserves and nature centers.

SAFARI

Motor Bikes Import, 6007 South Rte. 130, Pennsauken, New Jersey 08105, manufactures Safari motorized bicycles in Italy. The company imports them, modifies them to meet federal standards, carries out any modifications required by a particular state and retails the units through a dealer network covering most of the country. In business for about 11 years, Motor Bikes Import has produced mopeds that have been well received by consumers.

Safari mopeds are made in three models—The Fox, The Super Extra and The Shadow. Each has distinctive characteristics and differs appreciably in appearance and mechanics.

The Fox

The Fox is truly a motor-assisted bicycle and is a dual-purpose machine. Although all mopeds must have pedals, the Safari Fox more closely fits the definition of motor-assisted bicycle than most others. Instead of the 100 pounds or so that most mopeds weigh, The Fox carries a dry weight of only 69 pounds. Construction is tubular steel with integral fuel tank and baked enamel finish. The unit has a 48 cc Rover two-cycle engine, fueled with a mixture of 95 percent regular gasoline and 5 percent oil, delivering at least 150 mpg. The engine is mounted on the front fork and drives the front wheel by friction roller. Other features include automatic clutch, front and rear drum brakes, built-in generator, high-low beam headlight, tail and brake light, kick stand, tool kit, heavy-duty wheel rims and stainless steel fenders.

The Safari Fox.

The Safari Super.

The Super Extra

The Super Extra has a Minarelli, two-cycle, 49.6 cc engine with forced air cooling, automatic oil clutch and a Dell'Orto carburetor. The maximum speed is 25 mph. The unit has motorcycle-type shock absorbers on front and rear wheels, front and rear drum brakes, all-welded tubular steel frame with integral fuel tank, tool kit, kick stand, headlight with high-low beams, stop-tail lights, speedometer, heavy-duty wheel rims and stainless steel fenders. The unit delivers about 150 mpg. Dry weight is 95 pounds.

The Shadow

The Shadow has an all-welded, tubular steel frame, with a detachable three-quart fuel tank, tubular triple-chromed exhaust muffler, sealed beam high-low headlight, large tail-stop light, front and rear shock absorbers and drum brakes, heavy-duty wheel rims and stainless steel fenders, speedometer, a Minarelli single-chain, two-cycle, 49.6 cc engine with forced air cooling, automatic oil clutch and a Dell'Orto carburetor governed for 25 mph. The unit weight is 95 pounds.

SOLEX 4600

The Solex 4600 is imported by Velosolex America, Ltd., 86 Orchard Street, Hackensack, New Jersey 07601, a subsidiary of Motobecane. The unit has a single-cylinder, two-stroke, 49 cc engine mounted on the front fork directly above the front wheel. Transmission is via a friction roller that bears on the front tire and spins the wheel; it has a centrifugal, dry-operating clutch.

The frame features an integral, 0.34-gallon tank and fixed forks. The engine uses a mixture of 25:1 gasoline to oil (SAE20/30). Front brakes are of the rim type, with a drum brake on the rear wheel. Ignition and lighting are by magneto.

The unit weighs 68 pounds and delivers up to 200 miles per gallon. It has a sealed beam headlight, tail-stop light, luggage carrier and engine kill switch.

The front engine type of motorized bicycle was the first of the power-assisted bicycles. Some companies use electric motors and there are small electric and internal combustion motors on the market that can be mounted onto a regular bicycle.

The Solex 4600.

Safety authorities do not feel these motors, mounted on bicycle front wheel forks, and mopeds that have front wheel drive motors are as safe as those that have the motor located in the pedal crank area because they present a higher center of gravity and are not as well balanced. However, many thousands of this type of moped are sold annually in Europe and other countries, and they have been around in one form or another since the early Thirties. There are no statistics to suggest a higher accident rate. The Solex 4600 retails for around $300.

TOMOS

Tomos motorized bicycles are manufactured by the 40-year-old Tomos Koper manufacturing complex of Koper, Jugoslavia. The company is a huge conglomerate. The products include motorcycles, outboard motors, pumps and many more items, including Citroen automobiles that are built under license to the Citroen Company of France. Sales of Tomos motorized bicycles in 1976 exceeded 200,000 worldwide. The U.S. subsidiary, established during 1976, is Tomos America, Inc., P.O. Box 2030, 553 North Irby Street, Florence, South Carolina 29503.

During its first few months of business, Tomos America sold over 2,000 units across the country, mostly in the eastern states. Activities are now being expanded to include California and other states, and the firm anticipates sales of around 7,000 for its second year of operation.

The Tomos moped.

The Tomos A3S and A3S Super Sport mopeds seem to be built with the same degree of strength Jugoslavian technicians and production workers build into their rugged tractors and trucks. Most mopeds have to be pedaled along 20 or 30 feet before the motor takes over. Tomos mopeds, however, are started with a single backward kick on the pedals and then the engine bursts into life. The unit's motorcycle-type suspension features telescopic shock absorbers, front and rear, and a fully automatic two-speed transmission (no clutch—it shifts automatically from low to high at about 11 mph).

The engine is single-cylinder, two-stroke, air-cooled with a 38 mm bore, 49 cc displacement and compression ratio of 8.5:1. It has front and rear drum brakes, large sealed beam headlight, tail-stop lights, speedometer, electric horn, engine kill button and a one-gallon fuel tank (25:1 gasoline-oil mixture). The frame is all-welded with integral tank. The Tomos delivers at least 125 miles per gallon. The A3S model has a top speed of 20 mph to comply with regulations in states that have set this low speed for mopeds. The A3S Super Sport model attains 30 mph and is legal in states that permit this speed.

Chain lock, rear carrier basket, front automobile bumper rack, rear view mirror, windshield, etc., are some of the options currently offered. Tomos America, Inc., is marketing the units primarily through motorcycle dealers and bicycle dealers with the capability of doing mechanical servicing on these simple engines. The firm anticipates setting up a network of exclusive Tomos moped dealerships and service centers.

The units retail from $409 to $479 at present. The company soon plans to be importing a lower-priced model with a tubular steel frame, fixed forks and other construction economies that will not detract from the unit's basic ruggedness and reliability. The company anticipates selling this economy model at about $295.

VESPA

Famed Vespa products are produced primarily in the huge Piaggio industrial complexes at Pontedera, Pisa, Mortellini and other locations in Italy. Piaggio and Company has been in business for over 90 years and has produced two- and three-wheeled vehicles in the millions; airplanes, ship finishings, railway coaches, vans, marine engines, mini-trucks; and in 1967 Piaggio began producing Vespa motor scooters and Vespa motorized bicycles. In a daring move at that time, the company designed these latter products to appeal greatly to women. They were an instant success all over the world—a success that has not abated.

The company's first moped, the Ciao, is still regarded by many as the ultimate moped standard and is being made available to American buyers in several models. In addition, a new motorized bicycle was in production by the company as this book went to press, known as the Bravo.

The company's American affiliate, responsible for distribution throughout the U.S.A. of Vespa motorscooters and the various models of Vespa mopeds, is the Vespa of America Corporation, located at 322 E. Grand Avenue, South San Francisco, California 94080. Other factories and distribution facilities are located in Spain, France, Switzerland, Germany, the Far East, Africa, Central and South America, with many licensed affiliates in other countries. Annual production is in the range of 700,000 units.

The following summarizes the mechanical and other characteristics of motorized bicycles manufactured by Vespa and now being marketed throughout the U.S.A.

Bravo

Engine displacement is 49.77 cc, single-cylinder, two-stroke rotary induction; transmission from engine to rear wheel is by means of an automatic clutch and trapezoidal belt. Fuel used is regular gasoline with a two-percent addition of engine oil, maximum capacity .80 gal., and the company claims 160 mpg. Standard on this unit is variable speed with centrifugal speed governor and automatic clutch.

Tires are 2.25 x 16"; front suspension incorporates hydraulic telescopic forks and helical springs; rear suspension features double-acting dampers and coaxial springs. Standard equipment includes variable speed with centrifugal clutch, speedometer, steering column lock, tool kit, chromed luggage rack and a button on the left rear part of the transmission to disconnect the engine and place the unit in the pedal mode. Also standard are sealed beam headlight and rear-stop light. A few of many accessories available for the new Bravo include rear-view mirror, hand pump and turn sig-

The sporty Vespa Ciao motorized bicycle, now available in the U.S.

nals. As with all Vespa mopeds imported into the U.S.A., the Bravo complies with all existing federal safety standards and specifications.

Ciao

The specifications are basically the same as for the Bravo, except for the following: maximum fuel capacity is 0.75 gal.; tires are 2 x 17". Suspension features a front end sprung fork. Standard and optional equipment are the same as for the Bravo; principal differences between these units are in styling.

MOPED ACCESSORIES

Since motorized bicycles have been used extensively in many countries outside America for some 30 years, it is natural that a great many accessories have been developed, produced and marketed to millions of moped owners throughout the world.

The accompanying list and photograph (courtesy of Motobecane) briefly summarize some of the accessories being marketed in this country by Moto-

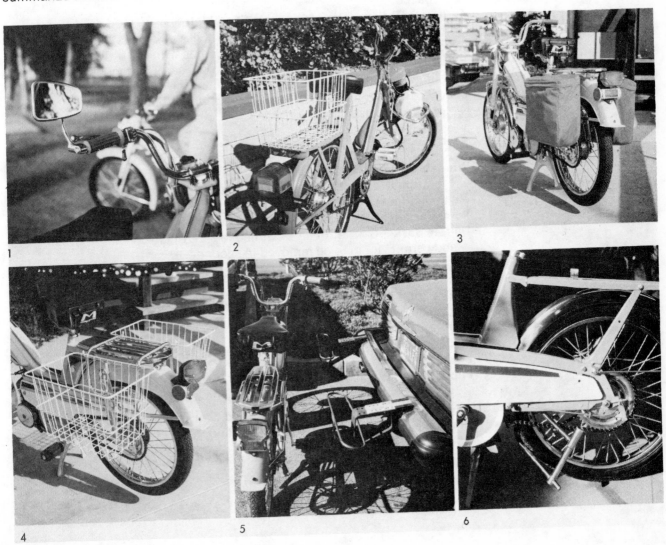

Motobecane accessories.

becane America, Ltd. Other makes offer similar accessories. The numbers on the list refer to those beneath each of the six photographs.

Some additional items offered by the various moped manufacturers and their United States distributors include: windshields; directional signals; case-hardened, vinyl-covered security chains with a variety of types of locks; audio theft alarm systems, wheel locking devices; snow-tread tires; rain-proof covers; rider weatherproof capes; picnic baskets, clip-on flasks; name and registration number plates; tire pumps; luggage rack security straps and rubber stretch cables; and various other accessories.

Motobecane Accessories

1. **Mirror:** Sturdy handle bar mirror folds away for easy storage. Convex lens gives wide view of road behind rider.
2. **Single Basket:** Single basket is easily mounted and removed. Available in metal or white vinylized finish.
3. **Saddle Bags:** Saddle bags fit all models. They hold their shape whether full or empty. Made of washable nylon, they are available in red, blue and tobacco.
4. **Double Baskets:** Double baskets fit all Motobecane models. A chrome-plated tubular rack carries the white vinylized baskets that are mounted or removed with a flip of a clip. This comes with the fitting for a padlock.
5. **Carrier:** The Motobecane motorized bicycle carrier attaches to the rear bumper of most automobiles and campers. Tie-down straps are available.
6. **Lock:** The Citadel lock comes complete with mounting clips for holding when not in use.

Below are listed some of the 1977 Puch accessories:

Windshield: Clear D.O.T. Lucite.
GN Custom Kit: Spring-loaded seat post and speedometer.
Maximix: Special 50:1 formula moped oil.
Puch Baskets: Vinyl-coated, large and durable.
Double Basket Carrier: Puch-designed rear carrier rack—holds two baskets and permits them to be removed in seconds.
Car Carrier: Port-a-Puch.
Puch Convertible: True cycling luggage, lightweight.
Puch Touring Bags: Exclusive for Puch with easy-on/easy-off design.
Puch Sage View: Rear-view mirror engineered for simplicity and low vibration distortion.
Puch Security: The Puch swing-arm lock.
Puch Cables: 6'5/16", 7 x 19 strand vinyl-coated aircraft cable.
Puch Clothing: T-shirts, caps, visors, Puch brand put-ons.

As moped use increases in the United States, no doubt many enterprising firms will produce more accessories and items of optional equipment.

3

Electric Motors
for Bike or Trike

There is understandably some confusion between a regular pedal bicycle (or adult tricycle), which has a small electric or gasoline-powered motor attached to provide power assistance, and a motorized bicycle which is a specially built vehicle incorporating either a two-stroke, single-cylinder, 50 cc (or less) internal combustion engine (or an electric motor). The latter is called a moped—motorized bicycle. The former is a modified bicycle and as such is subject in most states to legislation and regulations applying to bicycles only.

The purpose of this book is to present some understanding and knowledge of mopeds which, in order to be legally sold and used in the U.S.A., must comply with special National Highway Traffic Safety Administration construction, equipment and operating standards and with other federal and state laws passed especially for application to these unique vehicles.

However, to avoid further confusion between mopeds and modified bicycles, we felt the book should contain a chapter on bicycle conversions so that the differences between the two types of two-wheeled vehicles may be clearly defined.

There are a number of U.S. and foreign companies now making various types of electric motors to provide assistance for bicycle riders. The following presents descriptions of two approaches by U.S. firms that are rapidly becoming popular across the country. Before confining this discussion to basic specifications of the two types of bicycle conversions, however, the author wishes to point out the two main differences that separate mopeds from converted bicycles. They are: (1) The total weight of a bicycle with an add-on motor usually ranges from 30 to 50 pounds, including battery (if required), whereas mopeds weigh from around 70 pounds to about 110 pounds. (2) Mopeds, although capable of higher speeds in most cases, have to be governed down to 20 mph, 25 mph or 30 mph for sale in the U.S.A. (depending upon state requirements) in order to meet NHTSA standards. Converted bicycles, running on motor power alone, have a top speed of 15-20 mph. The two companies selected for inclusion in this book, and their bicycle conversion systems, are Electa Ride and Pedalpower.

ELECTA RIDE

Electa Ride is a division of Palmer Industries, Inc., P.O. Box 707, Union Station, Endicott, New York 13760. The electric motor kit for bicycles and adult tricycles marketed by this firm weighs around 8 pounds for the bicycle and 10 to 17 pounds for trikes. Since the average bicycle weighs around 25 pounds, and the lightweight battery only a few pounds more, the total weight of the bicycle, equipped with the Electa Ride system, is about 35 to 45 pounds, depending on make of bicycle, style, additional equipment, etc. The Electa Ride, running on motor alone, delivers a top speed of about 17 mph.

The differences in appearance between a moped and a bicycle with an add-on motor are immediately obvious—the modified bicycle looks like a bicycle with a small motor and battery added, whereas the motorized bicycle (or moped) does not look much like a regular pedal bicycle. Neither does it look like a motorcycle, motorscooter, trail bike or any other two-wheeled vehicle. It is a completely separate unit and is so sub-classified by the federal government and by those states that choose to follow federal rulings on the vehicles.

The Electa Ride was designed and developed by inventor Paul Palmer. Kits went on sale in the spring of '74 and were well received by an American public already being exposed to rumors of pending fuel shortages. Introduction of these electric conversion kits also coincided with the big bicycle boom.

Although many states now classify modified bicycles together with mopeds for legislative and regulatory purposes, some states have followed the example of the National Highway Traffic Safety Administration by creating subclassifications that permit bicycles carrying electric motors to fall under the basic bicycle regulations because of their silent and non-polluting operation and low maximum speed (considerably lower than that of even a three-speed bicycle). Incidentally, the Electa Ride company also is marketing a three-wheeled invalid chair, with electric motor drive, for handicapped persons—the unit has push-button controls. Electa Ride motors range from 1/4 hp to 1 hp, in both single and dual motor versions. Some models have commercial and industrial applications.

The electrically propelled bicycle concept goes back to 1897 when a patent was issued for such a device. However, electric motor technology was still in its infancy and the units did not become practical or profitable. Today's high-efficiency, permanent magnet motors and lightweight, rechargeable batteries have made these bicycle conversion kits useful and desirable.

Present limitations of electric energy storage capacity restrict the range of most electric motor modified bicycles and tricycles to about 15 miles—this can easily be doubled by using pedals at the same time.

Speaking well of the careful workmanship that goes into Electa Ride motors is the fact that the repair and warranty rate has been less than one-tenth of one percent over the three-year period of sales.

The company's 3/4 hp motor for adult tricycles with a Group 24 battery, delivers up to 40 miles on a single charge—again, pedaling will appreciably extend this distance. In any case, if you run out of electric power, you can always pedal home or to a telephone.

Major breakthroughs are expected in the near future that will vastly increase battery energy storage capacity, which will not only be of value to manufacturers and marketers of electric motors for bikes and trikes, to owners of these units and to companies building electric-powered mopeds, but also will be a boon to the practical development and use of electrically powered automobiles and delivery vehicles as fuel supplies continue to dwindle.

Installing an Electa Ride kit took the author just under 30 minutes, using

Paul DuPre

With Pedalpower, an electric drive attachment, any bicycle or tricycle can be converted to a moped.

a screwdriver and wrench—most people do it in less. The complete kits marketed by Electa Ride, including motor, battery, charger and fittings range in price from $150 to $250.

PEDALPOWER

Pedalpower is the trade name of an electric drive attachment for bikes and trikes manufactured by General Engines Co., Inc., Electric Products Division, Rte. 130, Thorofare, New Jersey 08086. Founded in 1946, this aggressive company now operates four plants in various locations and is the largest producer of this type of equipment in the country. The firm also produces construction machinery trailers.

The Pedalpower electric propulsion system for bicycles and tricycles consists of an electric motor, a switch, a drive wheel, a weather shield and a battery in a protective case. A special feature of this unit is a unicontrol lever which, when activated, automatically engages the drive wheel to the top of the bike's front tire and turns on the electric power that spins the front wheel. When the lever is released, the power turns off and the drive wheel disengages completely, causing no drag and thus resulting in no change of performance in the bicycle when in the pedal mode.

Since bicycles that have had electric motors and related equipment added (usually after the machines are sold) remain bicycles and are legally so classified in most states, they are not subject to NHTSA requirements for sealed beam, adjustable headlights, electric stop-tail lights, electric horn, hub brakes, and the five reflectors that are compulsory for mopeds.

Where motorized bicycles—mopeds—with internal combustion engines of 50 cc or less emit very little pollution, those powered by electric motors emit none at all. Owners do not have to mix gasoline and oil for the fuel tank. The electrically operated bicycles weigh considerably less than mopeds. The initial cost is considerably lower than that of the average moped —even if you buy a new bicycle and purchase the electric motor drive system separately. The conversion kit may be installed on any existing bicycle, men's or women's style, and when properly installed they do not affect your bicycling or the way the machine handles while you are riding, at least, no more than if you had a few pounds of books or purchases on board. The battery may be fully charged overnight on household current at an average national cost of about three cents.

These are the reasons why Electa Ride, Pedalpower and other electric add-on units now on the market are facing what appears to be a bright future from a sales standpoint. In 1975 over 10,000,000 bicycles were sold in this country and the total number of bicycles now in use is around 85,000,000. Meanwhile, although bicycle sales curves have leveled somewhat, they are still well on the increase, which appears to offer a tremendous market for electric power kits.

52

Paul DuPre

A common sight in European cities, commuters on mopeds can be seen in ever-growing numbers on American streets.

4

Mopeds and the Law

U.S. MOPED REGULATIONS

Mopeds in the U.S.A., like other vehicles, are regulated by the Department of Transportation's National Highway Traffic Safety Administration (NHTSA). NHTSA standards for these units cover lighting, braking, tires, controls and displays. In 1974 an important event occurred to moped importers, sellers and potential users. NHTSA recognized the growing popularity of and need for this type of unit in today's economy and environmental consciousness and amended its regulations in line with the special characteristics, speed limitations and safety record (in Europe) of motorized bicycles.

Thus, the moped was officially recognized as a separate vehicle and no longer classified with either motorcycles or bicycles. The amendments NHTSA enacted included deleting requirements for directional signals, reducing required stop-lamp photometric output to one-half that required for motorcycles, setting brake-fade requirements and maximum allowable stopping distances consistent with vehicle speed (maximum 30 mph) and permitting both front and rear brake controls to be located on the handlebars.

It was not NHTSA's intention to reduce safety standards, but, rather, to recognize that in absolute terms lighting and braking requirements for a 30 mph motorized vehicle cannot be the same as those for a vehicle with a top speed of 130 mph. Actually, safety equipment specified for mopeds (including drum brakes, sealed beam headlight and tail-stop lights) is in excess of that usually included on a normal pedal bicycle.

Changes made by NHTSA to its regulations have provided manufacturers and importers of these units the opportunity of making them available to residents of states where they have already been approved for prescribed use—subject to individual state regulations and to additional states that will undoubtedly legalize their use in the near future.

NHTSA also has paved the way for a truly economical, practical, safe method of commuting off highways for millions of Americans.

In addition, there are now strong possibilities of drastic reductions in traffic density, air and noise pollution, relief for some of our cities' overcrowded transit systems, ease of commuting, fuel savings and many more benefits to be gained as mopeds gain further acceptance and increased usage in U.S. communities. The economic impact of large-scale moped purchases by the public including servicing, rental, storage, garaging and insurance provides for interesting speculation.

Unquestionably, more U.S. companies will enter the moped manufacturing industry, and we will rely less on imports. This means more jobs, less valuable tax money paid out to the unemployed and a possible improvement in the health of commuters who use this combination of muscle and motor power.

These units also are being purchased for strictly recreational uses. Incidently, a recent study shows that despite their low cost, the average buyer is not the teenage consumer. One reason is that most states set a minimum age for moped riders at 16, and at that age most youngsters are thinking about cars or motorcycles.

Nevertheless, it is anticipated that the units will have increasing appeal for campus use, trail riding, picnic outings and club events—clubs are now forming across the country.

SUGGESTED STATE LAWS FOR MOTORIZED BICYCLES

[As prepared by the Motorized Bicycle Association]

1. **Definition**—A separate vehicle category should be added to the state code:

   "Motorized Bicycle"—a vehicle with two or three wheels, with fully operative pedals for propulsion by human power, and automatic transmission, and a motor with a cylinder capacity not exceeding 50 cubic centimeters that produces no more than 1.5 or two-brake horsepower, and is capable of propelling the vehicle at a maximum design speed of 25 to 30 miles per hour on level ground.

   NOTES:
   a. A motorized bicycle must always be capable of propulsion by human power alone *and* by motor.
   b. The maximum engine size and maximum brake horsepower insure the low maximum speed. Some state laws already enacted have selected a maximum of two-brake horsepower and a maximum speed of 30 miles per hour. This is appropriate for hilly terrain, since it produces better climbing capability.
   c. The requirement for an automatic transmission preserves the simplicity of operation of the vehicle and its controls.

2. **Operating Regulations**—State laws governing motorized bicycles should provide for the following:

   a. The motorized bicycle should be removed from the definition of "motor vehicle," "motorcycle" and "motor-driven cycle." Many of the "standard" rules pertaining to motor vehicles, motorcycles and motor driven cycles, under state law, are inappropriate for motorized bicycles. Specific operating regulations for motorized bicycle alone should be established, as follows:

   1. A minimum age for the operator—14 or 15 years is suggested. Given the simplicity of operation of the motorized bicycle, (pedals, hand brakes and no gear shifting) a driver's license should not be required. However, if the state wishes to require a driver's license, any valid class of license should be sufficient; if a state requires a valid driver's license, it is suggested that the law require any valid license or a motorized bicycle license

that may be obtained at the age of 14 or 15 by passage of the written portion of the automobile driver's license test.

2. Operation should be prohibited on interstate highways, limited access highways and sidewalks.
3. Registration should be as a bicycle, i.e., the vehicle should be subject to local and state bicycle registration laws. If a separate, statewide registration procedure is desired, it is suggested that (a) the registration fee be minimal (consistent with the main purpose of the motorized bicycle: economy); (b) the indicia of registration be a decal that can be pasted on the frame of the vehicle; (c) a procedure be established whereby the retail dealers (most are operators of small bicycle stores) can handle the registration process at their outlets, and forward the completed forms to the registration authorities.
4. Motorized bicyclists should be subject to all state and local traffic regulations and rules of the road.
5. Accident reporting should be required.

EXAMPLES OF STATE
MOTORIZED BICYCLE LEGISLATION

(THE FOLLOWING WERE AMONG THE FIRST STATES TO LEGALIZE AND LEGISLATE MOPEDS.)

	VEHICLE			
STATE	**ARIZONA**	**CALIFORNIA**	**CONNECTICUT**	**FLORIDA**
CC	50 cc or less	None	Less than 50 cc	None
POWER	1.5 bhp or less	Less than 2 gross bhp	No more than 2 bph	Max. of 1.5 bhp
MAX. SPEED	25 or less	30	No more than 30	May not operate at more than 25
REG.	Yes	Bicycle reg.	No	No
DEFINED	Ped. bicycle w/helper mot.	Auto. trans. req. op. ped. except if elec. powered	Bicycle	Moped under bicycle def.
DRIVER				
MIN. AGE	16	15	16	15
LICENSE	Any valid	Any valid or learner permit	Any valid	No
INSURANCE	No (fin. resp.)	No (fin. resp.)	No	No
HELMETS	No	No	No	No
COMMENTS	Law effective 9/22/76			

VEHICLE

STATE	HAWAII	INDIANA	IOWA	KANSAS	LOUISIANA
CC	None	None	No more than 50 cc	No more than 50 cc	No more than 50 cc
POWER	1.5 bhp or less	Less than 1 bhp	None	No more than 1.5 bhp	No more than 1.5 bhp
MAX. SPEED	None	None	No more than 25	No more than 25	No more than 25
REG.	No	No	Yes	Yes	No
DEFINED	Bicycle	Therapeutic bicycle	Motorized bic. or motor bic.	Motorized bic. auto-trans required	Bicycle, auto trans. required

DRIVER

	HAWAII	INDIANA	IOWA	KANSAS	LOUISIANA
MIN. AGE	15	None	14	14	15
LICENSE	No	No	Any valid or mot. bic. lic. at 14. No road test	Any valid or written only at 14	Any valid
INSURANCE	No	No	No (fin. resp.)	No (fin. resp.)	No
HELMETS	No	No	No	No	No
COMMENTS					Law effective 10/2/76

VEHICLE

E	MARYLAND	MASSACHU-SETTES	MICHIGAN	NEVADA	NEW HAMPSHIRE
CC	Less than 50 cc OR	No more than 50 cc	None	None	No more than 50 cc
POWER	Less than 1 bhp	No more than 1.5 bhp	Less than 1 bhp	None	No more than 2 bhp
MAX. SPEED	None	No more than 25	20	30	Less than 30
REG.	No	Yes	No	No	Yes
DEFINED	Bicycle	Bicycle, auto. trans. required	Bicycle	Pedals required	Moped auto. trans.

DRIVER

	MARYLAND	MASSACHU-SETTES	MICHIGAN	NEVADA	NEW HAMPSHIRE
MIN. AGE	16	16	15	16	16
LICENSE	Any valid	Any valid or learner permit	No	Any valid	Any valid
INSURANCE	No	No	No	No (fin. resp.)	No (fin. resp.)
HELMETS	No	No	No	No	No
COMMENTS					

VEHICLE

STATE	NEW JERSEY	NORTH CAROLINA	OHIO	RHODE ISLAND
CC	Less than 50 cc	None	None	None
POWER	No more than 1.5	Less than 1 bhp	Less than 1 bhp	No more than 1.5 bhp
MAX. SPEED	25	20	20	No more than 25
REG.	No	No	No	Yes
DEFINED	Bicycle	Bicycle	Bicycle, fric. trans.	Mot. bicycle

DRIVER

MIN. AGE	15	16	None	16
LICENSE	No	No	No	Any valid
INSURANCE	No	No	No	No
HELMETS	No	No	No	No
COMMENTS				

VEHICLE

STATE	PENNSYLVANIA	SOUTH CAROLINA	TEXAS	VIRGINIA
CC	No more than 50 cc	None	Less than 60 cc	None
POWER	No more than 1.5 bhp	Less than 1 bhp	None	Less than 1 bhp
MAX. SPEED	No more than 25	20	20	20 mph
REG.	Yes	No	Yes	No
DEFINED	Motorized pedal-cycle, auto-trans. required	Bicycle	Annual insp. pedals req.	Bicycle

DRIVER

MIN. AGE	17	None	15	16
LICENSE	Yes	No	Yes	No
INSURANCE	No (fin. resp.)	No	No	No
HELMETS	No	No	No	No
COMMENTS	Law effective 7/1/77			

NEW YORK REGULATIONS

New York moped legislation is not included in the above listing since two separate classifications are applied to moped operation.

First, the state classifies a moped as a bicycle and applies certain regulations. The state also classifies the motorized bicycle as a motorcycle and legislates its use in two classes. The following summarizes current New York moped legislative requirements.

[1] BICYCLE

Minimum age: 16 years
Maximum speed: 17 mph
One horsepower
May be operated on roadways where bicycles are permitted.

[2] LIMITED USE MOTORCYCLE

Class A
Minimum age: 16 years
Maximum speed: 31-40 mph
Treated as motorcycle
May be operated only where designated by Commission of Motor Vehicles

Class B
Minimum age: 16 years
Maximum speed: 30 mph
Any valid license permitted
No vehicle inspection required
$6.00 registration fee required
Protective helmet required
Mandatory insurance—$25,000-$50,000

Class A and B of category 2 impose most of the requirements for the rider as a full-powered motorcycle, but category 1 permits citizens this inexpensive, fuel-saving, non-polluting and short-haul transportation method, although mopeds are limited to the 17 mph bicycle speed limit.

The Motorized Bicycle Association is making strong efforts to bring mopeds, which are still quite new to the U.S., to the attention of those states that have not initiated any legislation to regulate motorized bicycles or their use. The M.B.A. has supplied all possible information to assemblymen, senators, state police, motor vehicle departments, highway departments, officials responsible for legislating vehicles, the press and others who are in a position to influence such legislation or are able to get bills initiated.

Many state officials fail to recognize the moped as a practical, viable and economic solution to many personal transportation problems, particularly as they apply to commuters.

In 1974 the M.B.A. prepared sample legislation and regulations based on the National Highway Traffic Safety Administration's recognition of the unit's modifications made to motorcycle legislation, for the express purpose of aiding states to understand the differences between various types of motorcycles and the motorized bicycle and the different regulatory requirements necessary to effectively legislate mopeds.

Several years have passed since the Department of Transportation's National Highway Traffic Safety Administration amended its motorcycle legislative requirements to make them more compatible with the low horsepower, speed and different uses of the motorized bicycle. However, a considerable number of states have so far failed to take the necessary action that would make the use of mopeds legal in their states that would help solve many transportation problems, as well as other problems associated with excessive use of automobiles.

Just before going to press with this publication, the publishers learned that eight more states have introduced legislation which, if passed, will make mopeds legal in those states, subject to their various regulations.

The eight states are: Colorado, Delaware, Minnesota, Mississippi, Nebraska, New Mexico, Vermont and Wisconsin. In addition, legislation was being prepared for early introduction by the states of Washington and Oregon.

If these ten states all approve the use of mopeds, the total number of states in which they will be legal will then be 33. As the year unfolds, however, it is a certainty that still more states will realize the many values of mopeds and will pass legislation permitting their sale and use.

CANADIAN REGULATIONS AND THE MOPED MARKET

In Canada, as in the U.S.A., mopeds are creatures of legislation. This is borne out by a review of the moped market in Canada since they were introduced in Quebec in 1973. Reviewing the Canadian moped market, we are primarily considering Ontario and Quebec since these were the first provinces to enact legislation that required operating conditions consistent with the characteristics of these vehicles. Nova Scotia and New Brunswick have enacted moped regulations in the past year but maintain certain motorcycle-type restrictions that have retarded sales.

The Canadian Moped Council's legislative program is based on the following viewpoints:

• A moped is not a motorcycle. The majority of legislators and departmental staff have never seen or operated a moped. They have heard about motorcycles and usually have preconceived notions about moped regulation.

• It is vital that definition of mopeds reflect all of their essential characteristics. It is also vital that operating conditions that are established be consistent with the definition.

The Motorcycle & Moped Industry Council, headquartered in Toronto, has had discussions and made presentations to legislators including the following information:

Definition
(a) Maximum speed not to exceed 30 mph.
(b) Maximum engine size not to exceed 50 cc piston displacement or electric power.
(c) Fully operative pedals mandatory.
(d) Fully automatic clutch mandatory.

Operating Conditions
(a) The minimum age is 16 years.
(b) Vehicle registration is required.

(c)   Driver licensing requirements must be kept minimal, such as:
1. Moped license on basis of sight test and proof of knowledge of rules of road; or
2. A valid auto or motorcycle license should permit anyone to operate a moped.
(d)   Only third party liability insurance should be required.
(e)   No passengers are allowed.
(f)   Mopeds are not permitted on limited access highways.
(g)   A helmet is not required.

As a rule, helmets are not mentioned, but if the government requires use of helmets by moped riders, the industry insists on a lightweight standard, consistent with the low speed and characteristics of mopeds, insuring maximum hearing, vision and comfort.

These points have been the crux of the Council's program on mopeds for three years. The council stresses the vehicle's simplicity and stability and points to a long tradition of successful, safe use in Europe and other countries.

THE CANADIAN MOPED MARKET

The Canadian market for mopeds is relatively small at present and, as characterized by the Canadian system of confederation, is heterogeneous. While buyers and buying habits differ, there is a common denominator linking consumer resistance to buying mopeds—overly restrictive and unclear regulations that result from an incorrect definition of "moped." This affects insurance rates, causes confusion through the dealer network and turns off consumers.

Canada's total marketplace is some 22,000,000 consumers. The selling season for motorized bicycles is similar to that of the northern half of the U.S.A.

Market experiences in Quebec and Ontario, and other provinces, are reviewed below.

Quebec Market

Mopeds were introduced to Canada through this market. Quebec is culturally distinctive because of its French heritage. The legal system rests on the Civil Code whereas the other provinces follow the Common Law tradition. Perhaps these traditions are part of the reason why French manufacturers introduced mopeds to this market in 1973-74. The first lucrative moped selling year was 1974, when some 30,000 units were sold.

Mopeds were then sold primarily through motorcycle dealers and exclusive moped stores. Department stores and corner store type merchandising exists, but has not proven successful.

The Ministry of Transport, Quebec, carefully studied the European approach to moped regulation in 1972-73 and was receptive to discussion with the industry acknowledging that mopeds constituted a separate vehicle class for regulative purposes from those now existing. Their regulations included: *50 cc engine* limit, piston or electric powered; *minimum operating age 14 years* with written parental permission carried on the operator's person if less than 16; *maximum speed 30 mph; excluded from limited access highways.* In general, mopeds were policed as bicycles. This fact resulted in numerous complaints, particularly from police groups who wanted tighter controls. Nevertheless, the moped market flourished and attracted dozens of brands, the majority of which originated in Europe. Major Japanese motorcycle manufacturers were also interested in the success of mopeds in Canada, specifically Quebec.

During 1974, Quebec's Ministry of Transport was working on Bill 45 (Appendix A-1). While distinctive moped characteristics were maintained they were brought into the Vehicle Code for the purpose of licensing, registration, vehicle standards, etc. The minimum age remained 14 years. When insurance was introduced, however, coupled with all the necessary formalities, one could no longer walk into a dealership, buy a moped and drive it home.

Insurance traditionally has been expensive in Quebec. Mopeds were a new phenomenon to insurers. Without a statistical history, their thinking was that the units were small motorcycles. Rates were established accordingly. Insurers discounted the European experience and consequently considered European rates as inapplicable.

The moped was no longer considered a bicycle from the standpoint of traffic control. Public enthusiasm for and acceptance of economical, fun and easy to acquire transportation was blunted by legislative obstacles. Insurance, for many, added a prohibitive cost; use controls and equipment regulations not only exacted a higher standard, but were not always interpreted, applied or enforced uniformly or correctly. There was confusion not only among consumers but also in dealer ranks.

Part of the reason for inconsistent interpretation is the fact that one Ministry writes the legislation and is responsible for its legal interpretation while another acts as enforcer (i.e., Solicitor General, Ministry of Transport). Quebec is a vast province; Bill 45 is but a small part of a total revision of their vehicle code.

Young people apparently caused the moped boom in 1974. When all that was required for a 14-year-old to drive a motorized vehicle was a mere note from a parent, it is likely that such notes were freely written. However, with the requirement of insurance and registration which increased cost and added a statutory complication, parents gave their written authorization less freely.

In spite of all the obstacles, mopeds cannot be considered a fad but, rather, a serious personal transportation alternative. The average public consumer now seems sufficiently interested in efficient, economical transportation so that restrictive legislation will not continue to deter moped purchase.

Ontario Market

As in Quebec, sales were primarily conducted through motorcycle dealerships and secondly, through exclusive moped dealers. Merchandising through department stores and unrelated retail operations, as in Quebec, did not prove successful.

Until Bill 177 was promulgated in February 1975, few people expected a major market in Ontario. The bill unexpectedly appeared quickly, permitting operation of mopeds up to 50 cc on 30 mph roads, at age 14 without license or registration.

Ontario consumers responded favorably to mopeds, which seemed to fill the need for a simple and economical means of short-distance transportation without parking problems and seemed easier and more comfortable than a regular bicycle. Many moped enthusiasts felt that cars should pay higher tolls and parking in certain areas where mopeds could be more efficiently utilized. It is little wonder that the initial sales surge was to older people in smaller communities for use as basic transportation.

Rumors of pending restrictive moped legislative amendments emerged from the Ministry of Transportation causing an immediate reduction in sales.

Bill 129 was slated for 1976 implementation. Confusion ensued since various sections were proposed for implementation at different times with no specific dates. The uncertainty that prevailed prior to the bill's promulgation still continues. The Bill raised the moped riding age to 16, required vehicle licensing, driver licensing, insurance coverage (including medical benefits), limited vehicle weight to 120 pounds, indicated a helmet requirement at a future date, etc. In fact, the government intended to implement motorcycle regulations but, after continuous pressure, decided against them.

Ontarians were quick to take advantage of the economy and the ease of operation of the motorized bicycle. The government did not expect the 1975 sales surge and made reference to the dramatic impact of the snowmobile on the market that occurred without controls, which caused public concern and criticism. By implementing Bill 129, the government felt it could be judged at the polls fairly since it publicly had admitted that Bill 177 was a mistake.

Other Provinces

Nova Scotia, New Brunswick and Prince Edward Island have enacted moped regulations that are generally restrictive. Throughout 1976 the Council worked towards developing regulations consistent with the characteristics of mopeds and changing regulations that were unnecessarily restrictive.

COUNCIL CONCLUSIONS

The Motorcycle and Moped Industry Council has formed the following conclusions and recommendations:

- Mopeds are not motorcycles, nor are they pedal bicycles.
- Consumers want and need easy-to-operate, economical transportation.
- Restrictive regulations are inconsistent with the characteristics of mopeds.
- To have no regulations would be inconsistent with our society's character.
- The benefit of unduly restrictive regulations, no matter how well intended, do not equal the benefits derived from widespread moped use.
- Mopeds do not discriminate against age (the oldest regular moped operator on record in Ontario is 79 years of age).
- Government representation must be made through a unified industry.
- The majority of moped sales are through motorcycle dealerships or exclusive moped franchises. Department store selling has not been successful so far.
- Reasonable legislation can only be achieved by a unified industry approach. Individual manufacturers and distributors tend to legislatively market only their brand.
- While the Canadian legislative experience has not been steady, there does exist a feeling of cautious optimism.
- In conclusion, the combined Canadian and American markets promise unlimited potential, if the many regulatory problems existing in both countries can be solved.

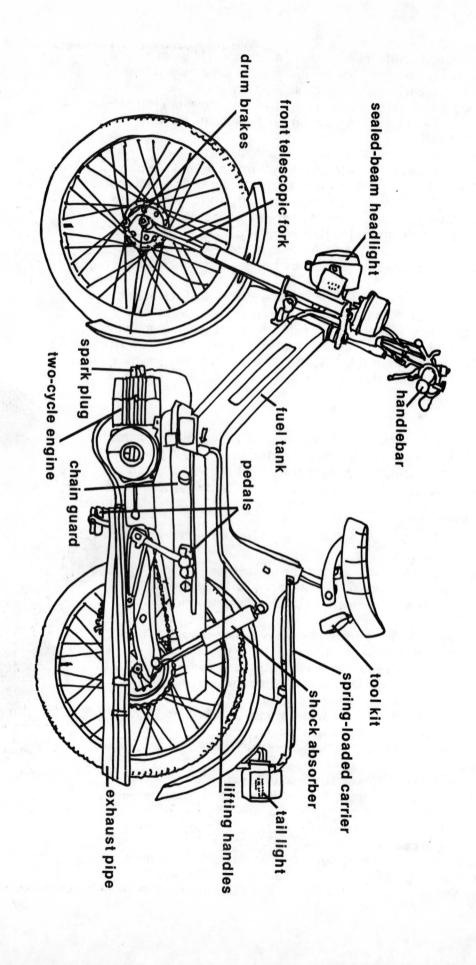

drum brakes

front telescopic fork

sealed-beam headlight

handlebar

spark plug

two-cycle engine

chain guard

fuel tank

pedals

shock absorber

spring-loaded carrier

tool kit

tail light

lifting handles

exhaust pipe

5

Mechanics,
Specifications
and Maintenance

The Motorized Bicycle Association, headquartered in Washington D.C., suggests that for legislation and regulatory purposes, mopeds be included within the definition of "bicycle" and excluded from the definitions of "motorcycle" or "motor-scooter." The MBA's official description of mopeds is:

> "Bicycles that may be propelled by human power or helper motor, with a motor rated at no more than 1.5 brake horsepower, a cylinder capacity not exceeding 50 cubic centimeters, an automatic transmission and capable of a maximum design speed of no more than 25 mph. A pedal bicycle with a helper motor may not be operated on the public roads by anyone under the age of 14 years."

Mopeds go to those out-of-the-way spots.

FEDERAL SPECIFICATIONS

U.S. federal standards applying to mopeds are stricter than those of any other country. One important requirement is that every unit sold must bear a certification label, either riveted or otherwise permanently affixed so that it cannot be removed without being destroyed or defaced. The label must be affixed to the structure as close as possible to the intersection of the steering post with the handlebars. The label must bear the following information:

1. The name of the manufacturer.
2. The month and year of manufacture.
3. The gross vehicle weight rating (GVWR).
4. The gross axle weight rating for front and rear axles (GAWR).
5. The vehicle identification number.
6. The classification type.
7. The required statement of conformance to federal standards.

The following is a typical example of the type of motorized bicycle certification label that the buyer should look for and should be checked carefully.

MANUFACTURED BY
ABC MOTORIZED BICYCLE CO., INC.
January, 1977

GVWR 253
GAWR FRONT 93
GAWR REAR 160

THIS VEHICLE CONFORMS TO ALL APPLICABLE
FEDERAL MOTOR VEHICLE SAFETY STANDARDS
IN EFFECT ON THE DATE OF MANUFACTURE
SHOWN ABOVE.

VEHICLE IDENTIFICATION NUMBER 0001
MOTOR DRIVEN CYCLE

In order to qualify for this federal standards certification label, each unit must conform to the following:

A. LIGHTS

Item Required	Requirement	
Head Lamp	One White	Must pass moisture, corrosion, vibration and recession tests: in effect, sealed-beam headlamp is only practical way to conform. If there is no sealed beam, there should be an AAMVA* Certificate of Approval.
	Aiming Adjustment	Headlamp must move up and down.
Tail Lamp	One Red	Should be a combination stop-tail lamp. Must be identified by SAE** Number. Must have double-filament bulb.
Stop Lamp	One Red	Stop lamp must be activated by either hand brake.
Reflectors	Two Amber Three Red	Amber on both sides at front (2). Red on both sides at rear (2). One red on back. All reflectors must be permanently affixed and identified by SAE Number.

 * AAMVA—American Association of Motor Vehicle Administrators.
** SAE—Society of Automotive Engineers (establishes testing values for components).

B. BRAKES

In order to meet federal braking performance standards almost all motorized bicycles will need drum brakes. To check the lining thickness of the drum brake shoe, an "inspection window" must be provided in the brake-backing plate.

C. TIRES

Each tire must have at least six treadwear indicators so that it may be inspected to determine whether the tire has worn to a thread depth of 1/16 inch. Some specific markings must appear on the tire:

1. The symbol DOT. (Department of Transportation)
2. A coded tire identification number.

3. The tire size in inches.
4. The maximum load rating in pounds and corresponding inflation pressure in p.s.i. (for example, 220 pounds, at 35 p.s.i.).
5. The speed restriction of the tire (for example, maximum speed, 30 mph).
6. The number of plies and cord composition.
7. The word "tubeless" or "tube type," as applicable.
8. A letter designating the load range (most often Code B— must sustain 300 pounds per tire.

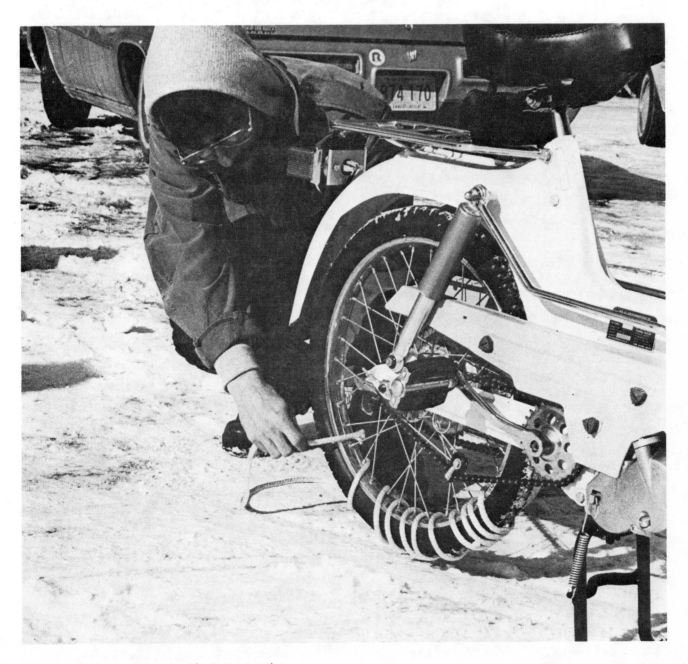

Wrapping cord around the wheel for better traction.

Checking the air in moped tires.

Filling the tires with air.

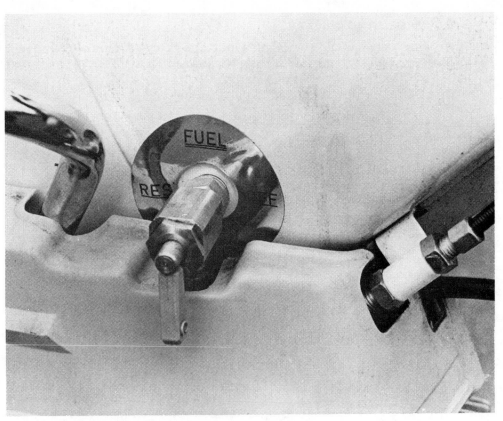

Fuel tap, set at reserve tank position.

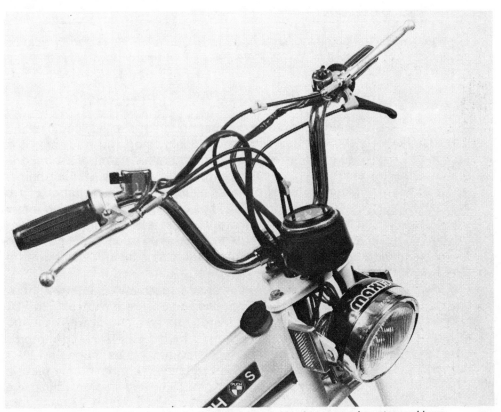

Front view of the Puch Maxi, showing headlight, hand brakes, speedometer and horn.

D. CONTROLS AND DISPLAYS

There must be two engine stops on a motorized bicycle. One of them must be located on right handlebar. It must be labeled "ENGINE STOP" and must have "OFF" and "RUN" positions marked.

With the following equipment, these rules apply:

Item	Required Location	Required Marking
1. Horn	Left Handlebar	Horn.
2. Manual Fuel Shut-off Control		Fuel. "OFF" Control must point forward. "ON" Control must point downward. "Reserve" Control—if provided—must point upward. Positions must be marked as shown: ("Fuel" indicates tap)

Reserve

OFF   Fuel

ON

Item	Required Location	Required Marking
3. Manual Choke		Choke.
4. Speedometer		Illumination required when headlamp is activated. Markings must be in mph.

The above was contributed by Serge D. Sequin, Chairman, Motorized Bicycle Association and with permission reprinted from American Bicyclist and Motorcyclist.

How Does a Moped Work?

A moped is a two-wheeled cycle. It can be mounted, started, pedaled and controlled like a bicycle. It has automatic transmission and no gears. It is stopped by means of hand brakes. Although there are variations from one manufacturer to another, a typical motorized bicycle has a small helper motor that is a single-cylinder, two-stroke piston engine in the range of 1.0-2.0 brake horse power of no more than 50 cc displacement requiring a mixture of gasoline and oil. This helper motor is capable of moving the unit and rider in a general speed range of 18-28 mph, depending on the slight horsepower variation. A moped engine is considerably smaller and less powerful than that of the average powered lawn mower.

The vehicle has low acceleration, power and speed and is lightweight. A typical unit weighs from 60 to 100 pounds (compared with 300 to 700 pounds for a typical motorcycle). Another comparison is that while the top speed of a moped does not exceed 30 mph, even lower-powered motorcycles can attain 50 mph and the higher-powered models as much as 120 or even more. This comparison definitely establishes the moped as a bicycle with a helper motor. Compared to automobiles and motorcycles, the moped is significantly less noisy. Its noise level at 25 mph is 73 dbA, compared with 84 dbA for an average motorcycle and 82 dbA for a typical car.

Fill-ups at the gas station are few and far between with the fuel-saving moped. Most mopeds get an average of 150 miles per gallon.

Measurements were made according to Regulation No. 9 of the United Nations Economic and Social Council, Working Part; on Road Transport, WP-2.

The Federal Environmental Protection Administration has recognized the minimal air pollution caused by low-power engines by exempting all motors of 50 cc displacement and less from emission control standards.

In normal street traffic, the moped's 25 mph is usually legal and sufficient to keep up with the traffic flow—thus presenting no detriment to normal traffic patterns. The 1.5 brake horsepower/25 mph maximum allows the addition of the latest technical engineering advances to the motorized bicycle—the "variator," for example, enables the moped to maintain its speed on steeper grades without increasing the maximum speed of the vehicle.

Lighting and ignition are provided by a magnetic flywheel turned by the engine.

The unit has a centrifugal clutch, which provides automatic transmission and greater simplified operation. Motor power for most units is delivered by a pulley running from a motor mounted in front of the crankshaft to the sprocket, which drives a chain to the rear wheel. Some units (particularly earlier types) are powered by a friction roller driven by a motor mounted on top of the front wheel. The latter are usually less expensive units.

The gasoline-oil mixture that provides fuel and lubrication, varies according to manufacturer's specifications and should be followed precisely. Many units are designed so that the fuel tank filler cap may be used as a measure.

Most units have disc brakes, operated by a hand lever on the handlebars. Some of the more expensive mopeds have a motorcycle type of suspension on front and rear wheels to improve riding comfort. On others, the wheels are mounted directly to the frame forks as they are on bicycles.

A study of short-haul/commuter fuel economy of mopeds as opposed to automobiles, based on 5,000 vehicles, follows.

SHORT HAUL/COMMUTER FUEL ECONOMY
MOPEDS VS. AUTOMOBILES
[5,000 Vehicles]

	AUTOMOBILE	MOPED
Miles per year Per Vehicle	3,000	3,000
Miles Per Year Per 5,000 Vehicles	15,000,000	15,000,000
Miles Per Gallon Per Vehicle	15	150
Fuel Consumed Annually (Gallons)	1,000,000	100,000
Price Per Gallon	$0.65	$0.65
	$1.00	$1.00
Fuel Cost Annually Per Vehicle	$130.00	$13.00
	$200.00	$20.00
Fuel Cost Annually	$650,000.00	$65,000.00
	$1,000,000.00	$100,000.00

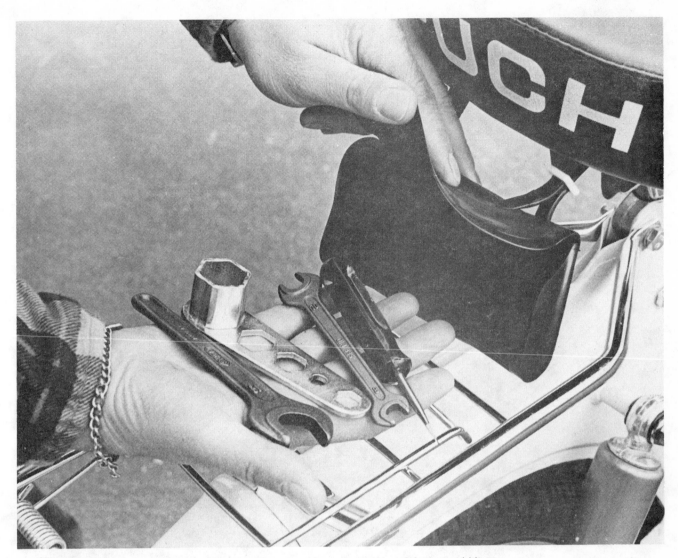

A standard moped tool kit, with wrenches and screw driver. On this model, the tool kit comes in a handy case that hangs from the back of the seat.

MOPED MAINTENANCE

Motorized bicycles require astonishingly little maintenance that include occasional oil change; a new spark plug two or three times a year; cleaning and greasing the chains; keeping the entire unit clean and free of dust, mud, grime, pollutants, road tars, etc.; keeping screws, bolts, etc. tight; maintaining tire pressures and other simple, common-sense preventive measures. Each manufacturer provides maintenance recommendations with his particular units. The internal combustion engine units require, for the most part, similar maintenance procedures.

Checking and Changing Oil

You should always check the transmission oil level when the engine is warm and the moped should be on a level surface. Remove the oil control screw (check your owner's manual for location). If the oil level is below the control screw hole, add oil recommended by the manufacturer to bring it up

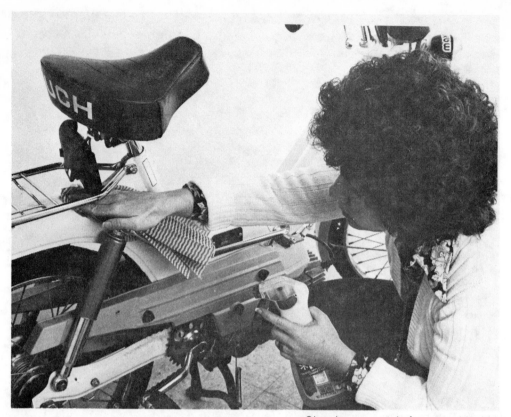

Cleaning a moped after a muddy ride.

Changing the oil.

to the right level. Transmission oil should be changed after the first 1,000 miles, and most manufacturers recommend a change every 2,000 miles thereafter. The engine is lubricated by the gasoline-oil mixture specified for each unit. The gas and oil should be well mixed in a completely clean container.

Calamine Removal

Calamine tends to form on the cylinder cover of most two-cycle internal combustion engines; it also may accumulate on the piston head and the exhaust port. Use a blunt object to scrape the calamine formation from the cylinder cover and the piston head since these surfaces are easily scratched. Before replacing the cylinder cover, it is a good idea to clean the inside of the cylinder with a soft rag and apply a light motor oil for lubrication. Completely dry contact surfaces between cylinder and cover. Be sure to replace gasket. When replacing the cover, alternately tighten down the locking nuts.

To remove calamine accumulations from the exhaust port, remove the exhaust pipe, then unscrew the spark plug and turn the motor until the piston is at its lowest point. Remove calamine carefully and avoid scratching piston or cylinder.

Cleaning the Air Filter

On some units, you get at the air filter by removing the intake silencer by taking out the locking screw from the silencer cap. With others, the paper filter is reached by removing the filter cover without needing to take anything else off. If the filter is not too dirty, you can usually blow off the accumulated dust. If the filter is heavily contaminated, it should be changed. The air cleaner cover should be washed in gasoline, wiped dry and replaced according to the directions in your manual.

Checking the air filter.

Maintaining the Carburetor

The carburetor jet should be cleaned out only with compressed air, and since the average moped owner does not have easy access to compressed air, it is best to have the carburetor cleaned by a moped serviceman. If you do have an air hose, first shut off the fuel valve, remove the cover and the air cleaner. Follow your manual for directions on removing the carburetor from the intake adapter. Take out the float housing and unscrew the main jet and the needle jet. Clean out the jet bores with compressed air—never use a metal tool, wire, needle, etc. Clean the float housing, filter screen and carburetor housing in gasoline. The carburetor must be replaced carefully to insure that the jets are properly aligned and the seals properly fitted. To adjust the carburetor, you should have the engine at normal operating temperature. Follow your manual since there are several different kinds of carburetors used by moped manufacturers. Units that have centrifugal clutches require special care, because if the idle speed is too high, the clutch will engage. It is probably best to have your carburetor cleaned and adjusted by a moped serviceman.

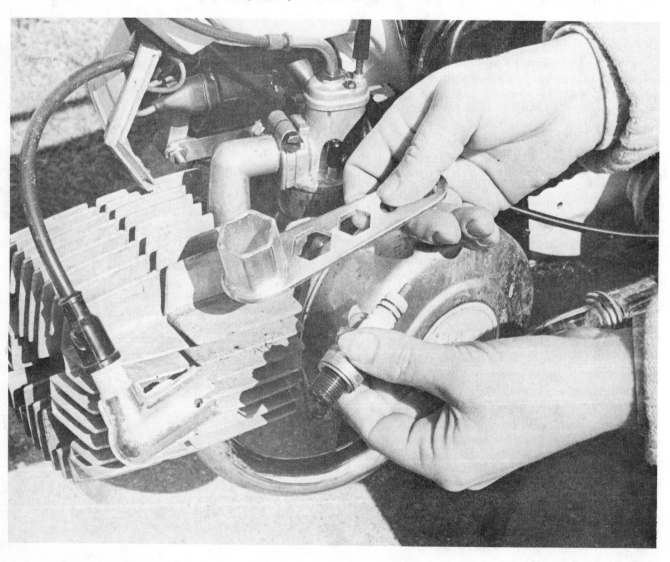

Checking the spark plug.

Cleaning and Replacing Spark Plug

Most moped spark plugs should be cleaned about once every 500 miles, of-
tener if necessary. Unscrew the plug, place plug connector with threads
against a ground (cylinder head). Operate the starter. There should be a
strong spark. Normal gap is .020-inch on most moped plugs. Clean the in-
sulator tip and between the electrodes. If the plug appears to be badly
fouled, replace it with a new plug, properly gapped.

Brake Adjustment

Brake cable tension and brake lever settings should be checked periodically and adjustments made if necessary. The amount of "play" in your brake
levers should be kept at a minimum. The "play" is the distance between the
lever when it is not being actuated and the point at which contact is made
between the brake shoes and the brake drums when the hand brake is applied. However, the brakes should not bind. Brake cables tend to stretch a
certain amount with usage that increases the amount of play in your brake
levers.

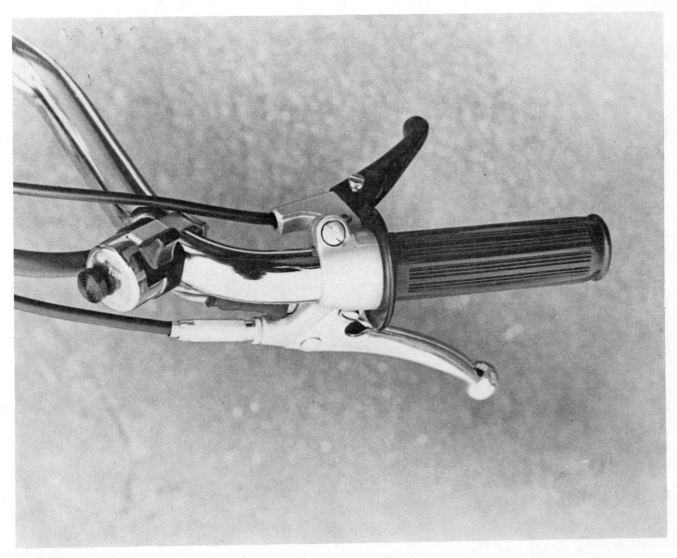

The hand brake

Although you should follow the manufacturer's instructions on brake adjustment, a commonly recommended method is to loosen the adjusting milled nut at the front of the hand brake lever, readjust the cable barrel, and retighten the nut. This slightly shortens the brake cable housing and therefore reduces slack in the brake cable.

Chain Adjustment, Lubrication

Some mopeds have a pedal chain tension device similar to the derailleur on a multi-speed bicycle. With this arrangement, a spring automatically maintains the proper tension on this chain.

To maintain correct tension on a motor-drive transmission chain, the following procedure is usually observed:
1. Loosen the rear axle nuts that hold the wheel tight in the forks.
2. Just to the rear of the axle nuts on either side of the rear wheel are the chain tension nuts. Turn both equal amounts—they force a bar against the ends of the rear forks that draws the wheel back, thus increasing tension on the chain.
3. Make sure the rear wheel remains properly aligned in the center of the chain stays.

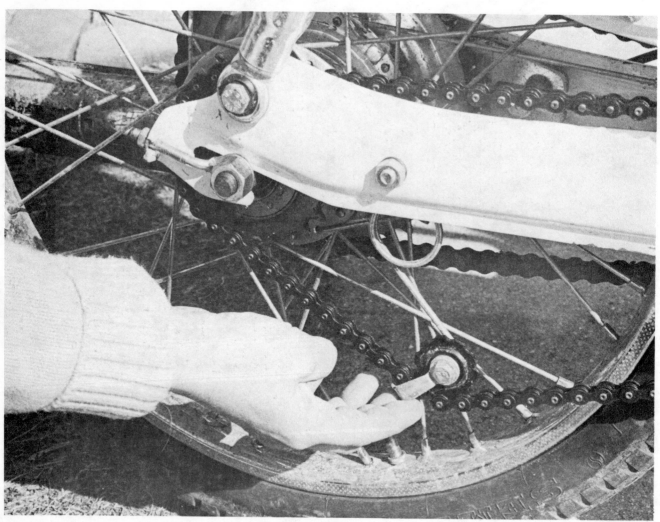

Checking chain tension.

Press down on the chain at the center point to check slackness. It should not exceed 1/2-inch (or as recommended by the manufacturer). After adjusting the chain tension, always recheck the rear brake and readjust if necessary.

Most moped manufacturers recommend the use of a 30-weight motor oil (SAE 30) every 600 miles in order to lubricate the crank gear bicycle chain, the motor drive transmission chain and chain tension roller. Any good lightweight all-purpose oil can be used for such points as control cables, the freewheel, and the kickstand pivot pin.

Every 6,000 miles, a good-quality, multi-purpose grease should be used to lubricate the upper and lower headset bearings, crank arms, pedals, front and rear hubs, front and rear brake cams, drive pulley and telescopic forks. Care must be taken to avoid getting lubricant on brake drums or primary transmission belt.

Servicing tasks beyond the general maintenance outlined in this section should be carried out by properly trained mechanics at dealerships handling your particular brand of moped.

Lubricating the control cables.

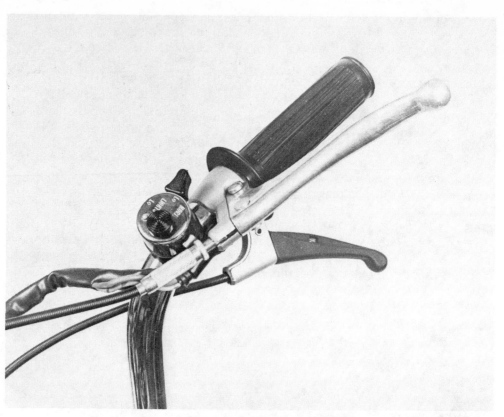

The switches for horn and light on one model's handlebars.

Regular lubrication for a longer life.

Mopeds can be squeezed into almost any parking space.

*The streamlined moped is not much wider than a standard bicycle,
and can be parked almost anywhere.*

6

Moped Safety

Safe operation of a motorized bicycle is, like a bicycle, largely a matter of common sense. A moped is not a toy. It is a practical, economical vehicle of considerable importance for the future of personal transportation in American communities. While it is a "fun" unit, affording pleasure to riders of all ages, a moped must be handled with proper respect for the machine, one's own safety, traffic regulations and the safety and convenience of others.

Mopeds do not have any special right of way—on city streets they are vehicles and have the same rights as, but no more than, any other motor-driven units.

Young people should be discouraged from "hot-dogging"—stunt riding —on the streets. One sees the possibility of the development of special moped tracks or areas where, after payment of admission or membership, those already proficient in the handling of their units may tackle obstacle courses or compete in other ways. Street racing, weaving in and out of traffic unnecessarily, riding on sidewalks, riding on the wrong side of the road and similar hazardous practices must be avoided.

TRAFFIC RULES

Mopeds must use the right-hand lane except when necessary to pass stationary vehicles, street repair projects or other obstructions. A moped rider must never ride against the flow of traffic, although this dangerous practice is permitted for bicycles in some states for some mysterious and unexplained reason. Riding on or near the center line is dangerous. An important point to bear in mind is that a person riding a moped does not display the visibility to other users of the street as does an automobile, truck, bus, etc. Mopeds have higher visibility than bicycles, especially at night, because of their sealed-beam headlights, tail-stop lights and the five reflectors permanently mounted on the unit as required by federal law. But, a moped is not as easily seen by other drivers as are larger vehicles. Another point worth mentioning is that in spite of the millions of bicycles and motorcycles now in use, American motorists are not as accustomed to two-wheeled vehicles on the roads as are motorists in Europe and Asia.

Mopeds are perfectly safe to ride by day or night, provided the rider obeys the law, acts in an adult and responsible manner, keeps his/her machine in good, safe operating condition, and keeps his/her attention on operating the vehicle safely and shows consideration for others.

Although rearview mirrors are not obligatory, they are available and advisable. At all times, the rider should watch all other traffic—and pedestrians. It is well to remember that a pedestrian struck by a 150-pound rider operating a 100-pound moped doing 25 miles an hour, is only likely to profit by the experience through a law suit.

The left-hand turn signal.

The right-hand turn signal.

The stop signal.

While motorists are usually careful to avoid opening the street-side doors of their cars without first making sure there is no other closely approaching car, many motorists do not take the same precaution when a bicyclist approaches. This could also happen with mopeds. In such a situation, it is better to slow down or stop rather than swerve out into the stream of traffic and create a potentially dangerous situation.

On city streets, mopeds should ride one behind the other, not abreast, and mopeds should not tailgate each other—the special hub brakes with which most mopeds are equipped provide positive braking.

Hand signals must always be given when turning or even lane changing. Hold the hand and arm straight out from the shoulder long before you start making the direction change. This helps insure the rider's safety by letting other drivers and riders know your intentions. This is the law. Turn indicators are available as optional equipment for mopeds—they are a wise investment.

SAFETY TIPS

Some inconsiderate people, particularly in suburban communities, let their dogs run loose, or dogs sometimes get out of yards. To many dogs, a person on a moped is fair game and looks like fun to chase, catch or outrun. The responsible, safe moped rider does not try to race a dog and should certainly never kick him. Kicking a dog from a moped can not only unnecessarily hurt the animal, but can throw the rider off balance temporarily and lessen machine control.

Moped riders should always be alert to children who suddenly dart into the road to chase a ball or one another. Children waiting at a school bus stop sometimes step into the road to watch for the bus. Adults often do this at city transportation bus stops. This is a hazard moped riders should be aware of and ought to be ready to deal with if it occurs.

Moped motors are very quiet, and people may not hear you approaching. This is particularly true of elderly persons. Often, people walk with their heads partially down to avoid a cold wind or rain. They would usually hear an approaching car, but might not catch the quieter sound of a moped. Many people are hard of hearing, and the moped sound is often beyond their hearing limits.

Physically handicapped persons, blind persons and careless people can present problems to the moped rider who does not remain fully alert at all times (this applies to operators of other vehicles as well).

In the city, there are special hazards. Taxicabs are perhaps the worst menace on city streets—not so much for the accidents in which they may become involved but for the countless accidents they cause. Many cab drivers are careful, skilled and considerate, but many others seem to feel that they are exempt from traffic laws. They will stop suddenly in the middle of intersections, in the middle lane, or just anywhere to pick up or discharge passengers, regardless of other traffic. They also suddenly swerve from the outside lane to the curb after spotting a potential customer—often without warning to other traffic, including approaching mopeds. Cabs frequently discharge passengers on the traffic side instead of the sidewalk side. Moped riders should keep a very wary eye on taxis. Fortunately, their distinctive colors and designs usually make most taxicabs highly visible.

Buses, too, present hazards. Bus drivers are often guilty of stopping in the driving lane rather than pulling to the curb to allow passengers to alight or board, as they should. If you are riding to the right-rear of a bus, this is a hazard you should watch for. Buses (and other motor vehicles) often fail to use directional signals. Buses behind schedule are among the most dangerous vehicles on the road. Sometimes they are manned by unskilled drivers often recklessly racing along, swerving from lane to lane, stopping on a dime, etc., in efforts to make up the time lost by their own inexperience and inefficiency.

In establishing criteria for the sale and use of mopeds in the U.S.A., the National Highway Traffic Safety Administration considered the fact that these units would not only be used in the daylight but also at dusk and after dark. Lighting and reflector requirements established by NHTSA illustrate the Administration's careful consideration of this factor.

EQUIPMENT AND ACCESSORIES

It is vitally important to keep lights in perfect working order for night riding. Even the daytime use of lights will increase your visibility to others. Wear light-colored clothing—a reflective outer garment is very visible. Apply pieces of reflective tape to your moped's frame, wheel rims and fenders.

Although in most states helmets will not be obligatory for moped riding and are not necessary for riding a low-speed vehicle of this type, it certainly does no harm to wear a bright-colored lightweight protective helmet. Besides, it helps keep your ears warm on a cool day and it looks sporty!

If you feel you need a radio along on your moped rides, it is advisable not to use an earplug or headphones or have the volume turned up so loud that you may miss important traffic sounds—like an approaching ambulance, or the corner policeman's yell for you to stop.

A moped's electric horn may not be heard by drivers of some motor vehicles, particularly high-noise-level vehicles such as trucks, buses, etc. It is therefore wise not to depend entirely on your horn to warn other traffic of your approach. The author, in road testing several of these units, found that a good technique is to use the horn when necessary and then presume the other driver or pedestrian has not heard it.

Always keep both feet firmly on the pedals when in motion. Dragging a foot on the ground throws you off balance, is generally unsafe, and it wears out a lot of good shoes.

A motorized bicycle is designed, built, and intended to carry one person. A passenger makes the vehicle difficult to handle, harder to stop, causes balance problems, and the passenger is in a very vulnerable position. Likewise, it is not a good plan to carry unusually heavy or bulky freight or luggage—this is not a pickup truck. As with a regular bicycle, one should avoid grating, broken glass, oily spots, potholes, etc., and take extra care crossing railroad tracks. Do not ride over the curb—this can cause damage and may throw you off your moped. Don't be a show-off—that's kid stuff—trick riding, riding without hands on the handlebars, etc. The folded-arms technique looks stupid and is unsafe.

As has been pointed out elsewhere in this book, there are many accessories and options available for mopeds. In addition, many accessories developed and sold for bicycles may apply equally to mopeds. However, moped owners should beware of carrying out structural modifications, such as replacing the standard handlebars with "goosenecks," or bicycle racing-type handlebars, etc. Do not change or relocate handlebar controls, nor remove the grips. Do not replace the fuel tank with a larger one, nor add another container for extra fuel.

New to the U.S.A. as mopeds are, already moped enthusiasts have their own magazine—Moped Magazine, Box 118, Bay Head, New Jersey 08742. The subscription price is $12 per year. The magazine makes available for $.75 a pamphlet containing an equipment safety check list and a list of safe driving tips.

As with any other vehicle to which you trust your personal safety and which you wish to keep in good mechanical condition (and maintain its value), your motorized bicycle should be checked periodically by a qualified moped mechanic at any moped, motorcycle or bicycle dealership that has one or more mechanics with moped training.

Steyr Daimler Puch of America Corporation—one of the American subsidiaries of European manufacturers who have done so much to get legislation passed to make it possible for Americans to enjoy the fun, convenience and economy of these units—has prepared a list to guide mechanics in checking and adjusting or repairing where necessary, all the mechanical parts on the average motorized bicycle. The list covers: engine kill switch, starter; head and tail lamps and all reflectors (including those on pedals); brake cables, levers, pads, and controls; front and rear wheel alignments; rear wheel spoke tension; steering head bearings; handlebars; seat post and adjustment; pedals and crank for wear, looseness, stiffness, etc.; front and rear tire pressures and wear; owner modifications that may have created a safety hazard; fenders; chainguard; kick stand; horn (and/or bell); turn signals (if any); general condition of frame, welds; chain adjustment and chain tensioner and security devices such as steering column lock.

The following charts present accident statistics for mopeds, compared with other motorized vehicles. These statistics are for France, Sweden, Switzerland and West Germany—countries where mopeds are used frequently. There is also a chart for Quebec, Canada, in 1974—the units are quite new in Canada. It should be kept in mind that these figures come from countries where mopeds have been on the scene for a good many years (except Canada). Injury and death rates are not given in the figures for France, since in the past moped, bicycle and motorcycle figures have been combined. However, they now are separating these figures, and soon we should have statistics concerning injury and death rates for mopeds, cars and motorcycles for France.

MOPED ACCIDENT STATISTICS

1. France

1971	Number of Vehicles	% of Accidents	Number of Accidents
Motorcycles	200,000	.0027	549
Cars	12,470,000	.00064	8,100
Mopeds	6,000,000	.00044	2,666

2. Sweden

1973	Number of Vehicles	% of Accidents	Number of Injuries	Number of Deaths
Motorcycles	45,000	.02711	1,180	40
Mopeds	425,000	.00419	1,681	100

3. **Switzerland**

   1973

Motorcycles	28,000	.08807	2,348	118
Mopeds	630,140	.00675	4,111	148

4. **West Germany**

[a] **Mopeds**

Year	Total Number	Number of accidents resulting in injury or death
1969	1,013.809	19.554
1970	1,052.543	20.670
1971	1,100.551	23.684
1972	1,223.991	26.017
1973	1,390.973	27.375

[b] **Motorcycles**

1969	265.000	26.458
1970	275.000	26.127
1971	285.000	26.829
1972	290.000	30.022
1973	300.000	30.175

Note: The number of motorcycles on the road is an estimate by the West German Association of the Bicycle and Motorcycle Industry. Actual figures are probably somewhat higher.

5. **Quebec, Canada**

1974	Number of Vehicles	% of Accidents	Number of Injuries	Number of Deaths
Motorcycles	150,000	.00918	1,337	41
Mopeds	30,000	.0053	156	3

The following conclusions may be drawn from the above incomplete statistics:

1. In France, mopeds are involved six times less in accidents than motorcycles and 1-1/2 times less than cars.
2. In Sweden mopeds are involved five times less in accidents than motorcycles.
3. In Switzerland, mopeds are involved 10 times less in accidents than motorcycles.
4. Because of possible inaccuracies, conclusions concerning West Germany are not drawn.
5. In Quebec, Canada, in 1974, mopeds were involved two times less in accidents than motorcycles. NOTE: In 1974 there was no minimum age for moped riders in Quebec.

Campers can switch from pedals to motor when the going gets rough.

7

Safeguarding
Your Mopeds

Mopeds can be stolen, just as automobiles, trucks, heavy construction equipment and bicycles. The latter are easy targets since owners often leave them in unsafe places secured with a single chain and lock that are easily cut. Bicycles are lightweight and can be quickly hefted into the back of a truck, van or even an automobile trunk.

There is no question that as moped popularity grows—and there are more and more of them on the streets—thefts will be inevitable. However, mopeds have a few things in their favor that, for instance, ordinary bicycles lack. One factor is weight. Mopeds weigh around 100 pounds each—some a little more. It is not all that easy for a thief to heft quickly into his van. Many bicycles are stolen by thieves who cut the chain and simply ride the bike away. This is difficult with a moped because of the steering column lock that is built integrally into the steering column and therefore cannot be hacksawed away. In this case, the thief can ride only as far as the front wheel is pointing. If you leave your moped with the front wheel turned as far as possible, the neighborhood thief can ride only in circles.

The thief has to remember to turn on the fuel, turn on the ignition, know exactly where the starter control is located and generally have a pretty good idea of how it works. He can pedal away once he has solved all the other problems, but these are not ten-speed lightweight racing bicycles and do not move along very fast under pedal power alone.

As with a bicycle, it is safest to use two vinyl-covered case-hardened steel chains, with the strongest padlocks on the market. Then, chain both wheels and frame securely to a permanent, non-movable object such as a lamppost. At night, always select a busy, well-lit street to park your moped —never in a quiet street with low-lumen lighting and never in an alley. And, never leave the unit longer than is absolutely necessary.

Make sure you have the unit registration number written down and with you at all times. As soon as you find your unit missing, call the nearest police station, give a full description including brand name, color, model, registration number, accessories and any other information that may help the police recover it for you.

If you live in an apartment building, don't park the moped in a rack that is not protected by a locked enclosure. If the garage has an attendant on duty around the clock, which most do, lock your moped up as close as possible to where the attendant stays—usually there is a booth or office. Make sure the garage staff know your moped is parked there, and ask them to especially watch it.

Having room inside your apartment or on a balcony is ideal for storing the moped. You can usually wheel your moped in and out of the freight elevator. Even inside your apartment or on the balcony, chain and lock your moped.

For extra theft protection, a moped can be taken up in the elevator and stored in your apartment.

Even if you live in a wealthy suburb or out in the country, never leave your moped unlocked.

If you use a public bicycle rack, be sure your moped is securely locked. If you are leaving it for any great length of time, remove any accessories that easily can be removed.

In many European countries, where the crime rate is less than the U.S.A., it has been found necessary to manufacture special racks with integral locks. These are coin-operated, such as a locker in an airport or bus station. The lock holds the front wheel to which you must remove the key. Even so, it is wise to use your chains and padlocks. If the operation looks too difficult to the thief, he'll feel the attempt is not worth the trouble. It is almost certain that this type of rack will soon be seen all over the U.S.A.

However attractive and useful a moped is, it is not worth much if used. These units cost between $300 and $400 on the average—car stealing is easier and more profitable. There are not that many around, and there will probably never be as many in this country as there are cars. A moped, whe - ther legitimate or stolen, attracts attention, so your chances of getting a stolen moped back are very good.

The best precaution you can take is to have your moped properly insured by a reliable company.

Safeguard your moped outdoors by locking a reinforced chain around a bike rack.

A couple around town on their mopeds, for the fresh air and exercise. (Photo courtesy of Motobecane.)

Mopeds can be ridden across fields (where permitted) and along dirt roads for quiet moments away from the crowds.

A moped rider cruises along a country lane.

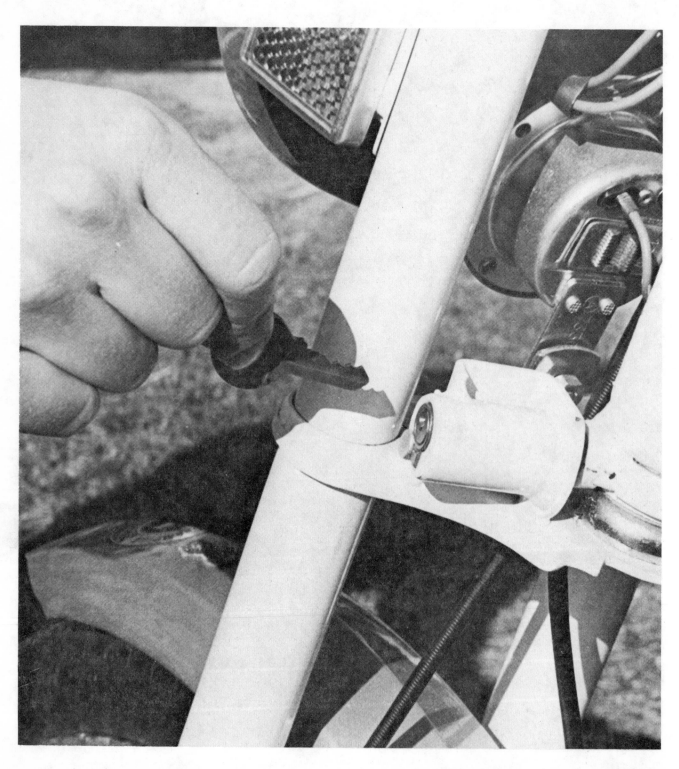

Locking the moped with the key.

Motor homes and other recreational vehicles take mopeds on vacation trips.

The moped's popularity is growing because riders can pedal for exercise or use the motor.

8

The Future
of Mopeds

There seems little doubt that moped use will be more common. It certainly has been a long time coming, as we are now about 30 years behind the rest of the world in discovering this answer to many of our personal transportation problems. Even though there may be no lines at gasoline stations at this time, we have been advised by oil industry and government authorities not to fool ourselves into a sense of false security.

The fact is that we are using oil much faster than our production. Due to the oil crisis, most Arab countries have become so wealthy that they no longer need the revenue they derive from oil exports. They have been investing enormous amounts of money in banks and buildings, industries and airlines, diamonds and gold, hotels and gambling casinos, motion pictures, stock markets and many other areas.

Ironically, a great deal of the money obtained by selling us the oil we need so badly at exhorbitant prices is now being used to buy huge tracts of land in the U.S.A.—in some cases entire resorts.

Fortunately, the U.S. government has been removing some of the restrictions it has placed on oil companies that has resulted in making it too difficult or too costly for the oil industry to carry out oil exploration projects fast enough to keep up our stocks and reserves.

Nevertheless, it is estimated that it will be at least 20 years before we can reach the point where we will no longer depend on imported oil for our many needs.

In the federal government, there are 64 separate departments and agencies dealing with the regulation of energy production, distribution and use. Most have regulated the particular products that are their special responsibility with little or no regard for the effects of their actions on the nation's total energy picture. The result has been a hodgepodge of rules and regulations that have caused the miring down of production and distribution of electricity, oil, gas, coal and petroleum. We now have severe problems that must be corrected before the balance between needs and production can be properly restored.

Ecologists, well-meaning, but often unknowledgable, have retarded the development of atomic power which could have solved all of our electric production requirements. Coal, the most abundant resource of all, is not considered an alternative because of anti-pollution regulations. Natural gas burns clean and produces high heat—ideal for the generation of electric power that is essential to maintain our industrialized society and our standard of living. Over the years, government price restrictions has made it highly unprofitable for private enterprise to explore and drill for natural gas or to be able to have it produced and distributed. Hence, our reliance on oil.

Protected by Raingear and guided by a headlight, this moped rider is undaunted by rainy weather.

The recreational vehicle of the future, mopeds offer nature lovers an alternative to bicycles and give backpackers a break from the hike.

A sign of the times: Mopeds invade the world of automobiles.

There is no doubt that internal combustion engines use a great deal of oil-based fuels. The automobile is a necessity in this huge country; trucks must ply the highways to deliver food and other essentials to our stores and buses must transport our people.

One problem we have had has been Detroit's practice of producing huge, bulky, heavy, gas-gobbling automobiles.

As the importation of cars from Europe began to become significant, many Americans realized that for a fraction of the cost of a Cadillac, one could purchase a Volkswagen or other import, which would give them triple the gasoline mileage at legal speeds. The imported car took up less parking space, less garage space, was better built in most cases and needed less expensive repair work, caused less air pollution and presented many other advantages.

Finally, between consumer demands and government pressure on Detroit to produce automobiles that use less fuel, domestic manufacturers have begun to produce smaller cars that give better mileage. Since many Americans have discovered the superior workmanship of most European and Japanese cars, they have come to realize the advantages of smaller autos, and have been purchasing imports. The result is that sales of American cars have slackened off—there are wholesale layoffs at the plants. In many cases, dealerships either have had to close or handle foreign cars, recreational vehicles and, in some cases, boats in order to stay in business.

At a commuter train station.

Mopeds take sunbathers to those out-of-the way spots that cannot be reached by car.

This brings our discussion to the moped that, at 25 to 30 miles an hour (legal speeds in most towns), can carry a commuter to and from work, a person to the store for groceries, make light deliveries, and perform many more tasks while delivering between 140 to 210 miles per gallon. Many studies of commuter habits have revealed that the vast majority of commuter cars contain only one person. For short commuter trips in good weather, use of mopeds by these lone commuters would save enormous amounts of gasoline. In many states mopeds can be used all year. Add to this saving the fuel conserved by their commercial use (as discussed in Chapter 1), and gasoline demand could be significantly decreased.

Paul Zimmerman is the executive director of the Motorized Bicycle Association, which has been studying the sale, use and effects of mopeds in a number of European countries for several years. Zimmerman feels that the moped is undoubtedly the commuting vehicle of the immediate future. He points out that in 1975 25,000 of the units were sold in this country. That year, very few states had set up regulations and standards for the use of mopeds and many were in the process of drafting legislation to this end. In 1976 the number of states that had approved the use of mopeds and had drafted rules governing their use, grew to 23. During the past two years, a number of articles have appeared in prestigious magazines, which has called attention to the use of motorized bicycles—usually for the first time. The result is that sales almost quadrupled in 1976 as 100,000 units were sold.

Taking the dog out for a walk with the moped.

The versatile moped takes this rider down bumpy gravel roads and deep into the woods.

The Motorized Bicycle Association has been carying out demographic and other studies of buyers over the limited period of time these units have been on sale in the U.S.A. The most interesting statistic is that most buyers are between 25 and 55 years of age. Outside of this span, mopeds have been bought by senior citizens living in retirement communities and by college students. The units obviously appeal to a very wide range of buyers—much greater than motorcycles, for example, whose buyers are mostly between 18 and 35.

As main factors in the growing appeal of mopeds, the MBA cites the ever-increasing cost of gasoline, the low initial cost of motorized bicycles (ranging between $295 and about $495), low repair and maintenance costs, bicycle rack parking and storage and the enjoyment derived from riding these units.

The Association also projects moped bulk buying—by resorts for rental purposes, by various businesses for light deliveries and messages, by large industrial plants for security purposes, by airports to enable personnel to get around faster than walking or using an automobile, by electric utility and telephone companies for line inspectors and many more.

Authorities believe that within five years, Americans will be buying mopeds at the rate of a million a year or more. The benefits to be derived economically, including the drastic reduction of gasoline use, will probably be far in excess of existing projections.

Reduced traffic congestion, exhaust and noise are some of the features offered by motorized bicycles. The low-speed, two-wheeled vehicles, which get 150 miles to a gallon of gas, are useful for short jaunts or for longer family trips.

A quick stop at the local bank is made easy with a moped.

The Motorized Bicycle Association anticipates sales of close to a quarter million for 1977 as more states follow those already permitting and legislating mopeds and as more dealerships open across the U.S.A. As 1976 closed, the 23 states where mopeds had been officially sanctioned had a total population of 140,000,000 people—a lot of potential customers.

As the word spreads and more states permit moped use, more businessmen will be encouraged to open moped dealerships, acting as distributors and importers, set up manufacturing facilities, open service shops, etc. Banks will be more amenable to financing the units, insurance companies will look favorably upon this totally new source of revenue, storage and parking facilities will spring up in towns—all of which will not only help the country economically, but will further encourage sales of these economical units resulting in still more gasoline saved.

The 100-year-old Columbia Manufacturing Company of Westfield, Massachusetts, the first U.S. company to manufacture motorized bicycles in competition with those being imported from Europe, believes strongly in the future of the moped for America. Columbia's huge dealership network will assure proper servicing of its units, and the company plans large-scale production.

Using the moped to get to a business lunch.

Tourists on mopeds are a common sight in Bermuda. Here, a family views the city of Hamilton across the harbor from Harbour Road.

Index